33 ⅓

EROTICA

T0001560

Praise for the series:

It was only a matter of time before a clever publisher realized that there is an audience for whom *Exile on Main Street* or *Electric Ladyland* are as significant and worthy of study as *The Catcher in the Rye* or *Middlemarch* . . . The series . . . is freewheeling and eclectic, ranging from minute rock-geek analysis to idiosyncratic personal celebration—*The New York Times Book Review*

Ideal for the rock geek who thinks liner notes just aren't enough—*Rolling Stone*

One of the coolest publishing imprints on the planet—*Bookslut*

These are for the insane collectors out there who appreciate fantastic design, well-executed thinking, and things that make your house look cool. Each volume in this series takes a seminal album and breaks it down in startling minutiae. We love these. We are huge nerds—*Vice*

A brilliant series . . . each one a work of real love—*NME* (UK)

Passionate, obsessive, and smart—*Nylon*

Religious tracts for the rock 'n' roll faithful—*Boldtype*

[A] consistently excellent series—*Uncut* (UK)

We . . . aren't naive enough to think that we're your only source for reading about music (but if we had our way . . . watch out). For those of you who really like to know everything there is to know about an album, you'd do well to check out Bloomsbury's "33 1/3" series of books—*Pitchfork*

For almost 20 years, the 33-and-a-Third series of music books has focused on individual albums by acts well known (Bob Dylan, Nirvana, Abba, Radiohead), cultish (Neutral Milk Hotel, Throbbing Gristle, Wire) and many levels in-between. The range of music and their creators defines "eclectic," while the writing veers from freewheeling to acutely insightful. In essence, the books are for the music fan who (as Rolling Stone noted) "thinks liner notes just aren't enough."—*The Irish Times*

For reviews of individual titles in the series, please visit our blog at 333sound.com and our website at https://www.bloomsbury.com/academic/music-sound-studies/

Follow us on Twitter: @333books

Like us on Facebook: https://www.facebook.com/33.3books

For a complete list of books in this series, see the back of this book.

Forthcoming in the series:

and many more . . .

Erotica

Michael Dango

BLOOMSBURY ACADEMIC
NEW YORK · LONDON · OXFORD · NEW DELHI · SYDNEY

BLOOMSBURY ACADEMIC
Bloomsbury Publishing Inc
1385 Broadway, New York, NY 10018, USA
50 Bedford Square, London, WC1B 3DP, UK
29 Earlsfort Terrace, Dublin 2, Ireland

BLOOMSBURY, BLOOMSBURY ACADEMIC and the Diana logo are trademarks of Bloomsbury
Publishing Plc

First published in the United States of America 2023

Copyright © Michael Dango, 2023

Bloomsbury Publishing Inc does not have any control over, or responsibility for, any third-party
websites referred to or in this book. All internet addresses given in this book were correct at the
time of going to press. The author and publisher regret any inconvenience caused if addresses
have changed or sites have ceased to exist, but can accept no responsibility for any such changes.

Whilst every effort has been made to locate copyright holders the publishers would be grateful
to hear from any person(s) not here acknowledged.

Library of Congress Cataloging-in-Publication Data

Names: Dango, Michael, author.
Title: Erotica / Michael Dango.
Description: [1st.] | New York : Bloomsbury Academic, 2023. | Series: 33 ⅓ | Includes
bibliographical references and index. | Summary: "Madonna's Erotica made the sentimental sexy
at a time when the gay community and American culture were both re-thinking the nature of
intimacy"– Provided by publisher.
Identifiers: LCCN 2023001419 (print) | LCCN 2023001420 (ebook) | ISBN 9781501388996
(paperback) | ISBN 9781501389009 (ebook) | ISBN 9781501389016 (pdf) |
ISBN 9781501389023 (ebook other)
Subjects: LCSH: Madonna, 1958- Erotica. | Madonna, 1958—Criticism and interpretation. |
Popular music–Social aspects. | Homosexuality and popular music. |
Sex and popular music. | Sex in popular culture.
Classification: LCC ML420.M1387 M24 2023 (print) | LCC ML420.M1387 (ebook) |
DDC 782.42166092–dc23/eng/20230113
LC record available at https://lccn.loc.gov/2023001419
LC ebook record available at https://lccn.loc.gov/2023001420

ISBN: PB: 978-1-5013-8899-6
ePDF: 978-1-5013-8901-6
eBook: 978-1-5013-8900-9

Series: 33 ⅓

Typeset by Deanta Global Publishing Services, Chennai, India
Printed and bound in Great Britain

To find out more about our authors and books visit www.bloomsbury.com and sign up
for our newsletters.

For Matthias

Contents

Introduction

Each year toward the end of summer, entertainment news outlets and websites have a time-honored ritual. It's called "Can You Believe How Old Madonna Is?" There are a couple of different variations on the ritual, commemorating the artist's birth on August 16, 1958. The first treats the question as praise: look at this Queen of Pop, this superstar who broke literally all the records, who gave birth by surrogacy to a generation of Britneys and Gagas, whose skin remains flawless, whose classics are iconic, and whose new music remains relevant—can you believe she could really be forty, fifty, sixty years old? The second version of the ritual is more incredulous in tone. Who does this Madonnasaurus, this mother of six, inevitably literally a granny, think she is still wearing those heels, thrusting those hips, pretending, desperately, to still be *pop*?

In 2022, this ritual had an update. A week before her birthday, Beyoncé sent Madonna some flowers and a note: "I am so grateful for you. You have opened so many doors for so many women. You are a masterpiece genius." But Beyoncé wasn't wishing her elder a happy birthday. She was thanking Madonna for permission to interpolate her famous "Vogue" single from 1990 into a "Queen's Remix" of Beyoncé's debut track from her latest album *RENAISSANCE*. The album acknowledges and extends the Black and queer origins of US dance music, much how "Vogue" was originally named after a dance style innovated by Black and Latinx performers in the underground queer ball culture of Harlem in the late 1980s. But this is where fans and Twitter critics had some new questions to raise. Since Madonna is neither queer nor Black, wasn't her song a form of cultural appropriation? Perhaps Madonna had "opened so many doors for so many women," but how many of those women were women of color? It's true that, even before Beyoncé, Madonna had been recognized by artists such as Nicki Minaj and M.I.A., but for many critics, her aesthetic choices tended to obscure rather than acknowledge her racial debts; when she performed "Vogue" at the 1990 MTV Music Video Awards, she donned an eighteenth-century French court outfit originally worn by Glenn Close in the period film *Dangerous Liaisons*. What made Madonna seem so old, this time, was not just that she had already been in her thirties when the house music that Beyoncé samples in her album came out. She also seemed old because of a racial insensitivity that itself seemed out of date. In the wake of racial reckonings led by Black Lives Matter in the past decade, this Madonnasaurus was a fossil from another era.

One of the things I'll argue in this book is that we should be skeptical of progress narratives such as this, like things are automatically better today than they were thirty years ago. But another is that it's precisely because Madonna has been around so long and at the center of so many controversies—

and I mean the *interesting* controversies, not the ones over whether she should wear a pointed bra but the ones over who owns the cultural materials she draws upon—that she both remains relevant and, even when stuck in the past, still has something to teach us about the present and how we got here, like all fossils do. The 2022 debate over Beyoncé and Madonna was itself a renaissance of controversies circling Madonna a generation prior, often orbiting her album from exactly thirty years before, the 1992 *Erotica*, which was her first studio album since "Vogue" had been released on the soundtrack accompanying the film *Dick Tracy* (in which she stars alongside Warren Beatty). In US culture and politics, 2022 uncannily echoes 1992. Then, as now, a global pandemic that, in the United States, disproportionately affects people of color and especially men who have sex with men grips the public imagination; then, it was HIV/AIDS, and now it's Covid-19 and Monkeypox. Then, as now, amid heightened cultural warfare and economic insecurity, a Democratic presidency was said to offer hope against rising religious fundamentalism and white extremism; in 1992 it was Clinton ending the twelve years of Reagan and Bush, Sr., and now we have Biden's post-Trump presidency. Then, as now, the United States is grappling with the ongoing legacies of police brutality, whether ignited by the spring 1991 Los Angeles Police Department's beating of Rodney King or the summer 2020 police murders of George Floyd and Breonna Taylor.

In the midst of the earlier period of heightened economic inequality, cultural conservatism, and religious fundamentalism, a period when artists funded by the

National Endowment for the Arts had their funding taken away for being too provocative, which meant too sexual and usually too gay, Madonna released not only an album called *Erotica* but also a pornographic coffee table book called *Sex* and an erotic thriller called *Body of Evidence*. Today, it's this sense of a cultural division, and Madonna's acute awareness of her possible place within it, that makes *Sex*, *Erotica*, and *Body of Evidence*—a trilogy that ended the artist's imperial phase of commercial and creative peaking—seem both out of time and of our current time. As we will see in later chapters, Madonna has *always* been both archaic and avant-garde, boasting a style that is promiscuous with time periods, fashions, and political movements—and this is largely the reason she is both worthy of praise and worthy of incredulity. Consider *The Girlie Show*, the video of the 1993 concert that toured *Erotica* and is therefore a summation of Madonna's sexual trilogy. When *The Girlie Show* was released on DVD in 1998, five years after it originally aired as an HBO special, it was one of the first on that platform. The scene that sticks in my mind arrives toward the end of the concert's second act, titled "Studio 54." Like the tax fraud-troubled disco nightclub that is its namesake, the songs in this act are mostly dance. Madonna enters sitting cross-legged atop a giant disco ball that descends from the ceiling. She's wearing a blond afro and then breaks into her *Erotica* single "Why's It So Hard," which gets her and her multiracial crew of dancers shirtless and grinding on the stage. As she sings the final lines—*Why's it so hard to love one another? Love your sister, love your brother*—the camera zooms in on her right hand, slowly rising with a clenched fist.

It's odd timing for the symbol most frequently associated with Black Power to appear, especially since she has not really answered the question of racism's origins (*Why's it so hard to love one another?*) so much as prescribed love as the solution with the command, *Love your sister, love your brother.* It's odd not just because it's a Black symbol in a white hand but because it's a symbol of 1960s political radicalism during a 1970s free love disco lyric being sung in the 1990s. This was a year after the police beat up Rodney King, and the disco floor sounds like a safer place to be, where love always triumphs over violence, where *Nothing really matters. Love is all we need.*

And yet, in Madonna's monologue that follows, it seems police brutality is not even the injustice Madonna has on her mind. What she calls "the greatest tragedy of the twentieth century" is the AIDS epidemic, which by 1993—more than a decade after the Gay Men's Health Crisis had formed in New York to care for community members suffering from a mysterious new illness but only half a decade after President Ronald Reagan would even publicly acknowledge the disease—had killed more than 100,000 in the United States, primarily men who had sex with men and primarily men of color. The monologue is an introduction to "In This Life," which mourns two close friends who had died of AIDS. Martin Burgoyne, her former roommate in New York City, *was only 23, gone before he had his time.* Christopher Flynn, her high school dance teacher who first introduced her to gay bars, *was like a father to me.* He *said that we're all made of flesh and blood, why should he be treated differently, shouldn't matter who you choose to love.*

After the monologue and before the song begins, Madonna, now alone on stage, raises her clenched fist once more. It's a confusing moment, this double booking of the clenched fist, this cross-purpose appropriation of Black Power imagery. It's that the fist has been deracinated not just of its historical context but also of its political method, a politics now not of militancy but of love. The crux of many tensions surrounding Madonna is this tendency to ignore context, something that can be both powerful and silly. In the predominantly Catholic Philippines, where my family is from, Madonna has enjoyed popularity because the provocative lyrics of a song like "Like a Virgin" or "Papa Don't Preach" provide just enough of a mainstream pushback against religiously sanctioned gender norms. But Madonna never performed in the Philippines until 2016, and when she finally did, she draped herself in the national flag, which is actually illegal. Here is a gesture toward national respect that is technically disrespectful, and it is as if Madonna may be more meaningful, may be more resonant with a fan base, if she is a little distant from them. Because with a little distance, a fan base can appropriate her materials for their own uses. A speculative interpretation of what Madonna means in the Philippines will always be more expansive, more capacious, and frankly more interesting than whatever Madonna, when prompted, has to say about the Philippines herself. In other words, the legacy of her music is mostly what people do with her music: the social scenes for which it provides a soundtrack, the cultural debates and dialogues for which it provides an occasion.

And debate, of course, is what she's usually after—to be the center of the conversation, whatever the conversation. In a documentary released a couple of years before *The Girlie Show*, Madonna explained how she saw herself on the global stage: "I know I'm not the best singer and not the best dancer, but I'm not interested in that. I'm interested in pushing people's buttons and being provocative and political." Here, "political" has become an identity, something one is rather than what someone does, which is why Madonna can do it alone on stage, instead of in the streets or on the picket line. The next year, in an interview with Carrie Fisher in *Rolling Stone*, the *Star Wars* star told Madonna, "You enjoy being controversial. That used to mean talking about things that were never talked about. Now, it seems controversy is just a diluted form of pornography or obscenity. I'm not suggesting that you do pornography, but you do obscenity."[1] It's not so much that Madonna knew sex sold. She knew controversy sold, knew how to make money off of "pushing people's buttons and being provocative and political."

In the context of *Erotica*, the flip side of caring more about controversy than sex per se is that Madonna's work, even at its officially sexiest, often has little to do with sex. The coffee table book simply titled *Sex* does but *Erotica* not so much. The book lives up to its name, which is simply imprinted on its industrial aluminum cover, inspired by post-punk band Public Image Ltd.'s 1979 album *Metal*. The book has penises and men in harnesses and accompanying text with

---

[1] Carrie Fisher, "Madonna: *The Rolling Stone* Interview," *Rolling Stone*, no. 606 (June 13, 1991).

statements like "ass fucking is the most pleasurable way to get fucked and it hurts the most too" and—both more interesting and less sexy—Madonna's then-boyfriend Vanilla Ice trying and failing to pull off a macho-muscle look from Tom of Finland. The book clearly wanted to be a key entry in the culture wars of the 1990s, and although most critics thought it tried too hard, too desperately to be provocative—the work of an aspiring teenage rebel who was actually thirty-four years old—it's undeniable the book's contents were in sync with its title. But *Erotica*, Madonna's fifth studio album and nearly a decade into her recording career, is one of the least sexy of her albums.

Instead, *Erotica* is sentimental. *Erotica* was Madonna's danciest album to date, and you're not supposed to go to the dance floor looking for love. At the end of the decade, Destiny's Child would put it best: *Ladies leave your man at home, 'cause it's eleven-thirty and the club is jumpin' jumpin'.* Their advice to the boys: *You're gonna find a sexy chica that's gon' dance all night if you wanna.* But the genius of *Erotica* may actually be how it found a way to dress up something very sentimental, something about desperately needing connection and community more than a hookup, in clothes that looked scandalous. This was great for Madonna, who wanted to sell albums, and of course it was great for folks like the Christian Coalition of America, who love to be scandalized. But it was also great for many in Madonna's core audience, overtly addressed by the album: gay men who had lost their friends and partners to AIDS. Sex was—is— an important part of gay identity, and sexual culture is one of the ways we reproduce ourselves by means other than having kids. Promiscuity is a stereotype, but it is also an ethic. The S&M club, the bathhouse, the backroom at the bar: these are cultural institutions, which means they are—like churches—institutions that sustain a culture, that provide a sense of belonging in shared practices (cruising rather than communion), aesthetics (leather harnesses rather than clerical robes), and even an upgraded set of "good manners" (it's tacky to blow someone in the front bar instead of the back). But in the midst of a sexually transmitted plague, what to do when sex is both desired and feared? And how to find physical comfort in a state of permanent mourning? As I'll explain in later chapters, *Erotica* provides one answer: make something *sound* like sex, when really it's about holding hands.

This book is an exploration of these cultural elements of *Erotica*: its position within the wider context of US culture wars of the 1980s–1990s; its response to the need for "safe sex" in a queer community ravaged by AIDS; and how it marks an inflection point as queer politics transitioned from emphasizing sexual liberation to pushing same-sex marriage. And it is a book about how these inflection points are captured in the album's tension between the sentimental and the pornographic, a tension lodged in its very sound: tensions between the spoken and the sung, between the analog (intentionally recorded album scratches) and the digital (synth-pop vibes); between the repetitious beats of disco and the melodies of pop (not to mention the bizarre "Did You Do It?" track included in the explicit version of the album with Mark Goodman and Dave Murphy rapping about whether they fucked Madonna in a limo driving through Central Park). If the erotic is supposed to be about connection, why does this album have no featured voices Madonna is in conversation with, no duets? There's always something inevitably oxymoronic about the erotic soloist: singing about sex only draws attention to the fact you're not having it.

Instead of featured singers, *Erotica* features instruments and intrusive sound effects. Typewriters clack, sirens wail, glass breaks—which, at least to me, would kind of ruin the mood. It was also the album that announced Madonna's developing interest in global music, from the plagiarized Middle Eastern scales in the title song, to the xylophone arrangement in her "Fever" cover that somehow comes off vaguely reggae, to the flamenco guitar bridge in "Deeper and Deeper." The overall eclecticness of the album—its uneasy mix of rap, jazz, electropop, hip-hop, disco, and, it must be repeated, flamenco—speaks to a kind of endless dissatisfaction with sex itself, or rather, the desire for novelty, for keeping it fresh. That a turn to "foreign" sounds is part of an Orientalist legacy—how passion is projected onto the Middle East or "Romance language" nations—is one of the things going on here, as I'll explore in future chapters. In the domestic US context, as Lauren Michele Jackson has put it in her recent book on cultural appropriation, Madonna is also among artists, especially Christina Aguilera, who "found a shortcut to sexuality" through consuming "not blackness but the *idea* of black aesthetics."[2] But in addition to cultural

---

[2]Lauren Michele Jackson, *White Negroes: When Cornrows Were in Vogue . . . and Other Thoughts on Cultural Appropriation* (Boston, MA: Beacon Press, 2019), 22.

appropriation, the other thing going on here is the inability to nail the erotic to a particular genre or to find a genre adequate to expressing the rhythms of the erotic in sound.

*   *   *

The Girlie Show is a name for a striptease, but the concert it videotapes only gives us forty-five seconds of stripping. What may be more memorable for some viewers is not the clenched fists at the show's halfway point but the topless dancer descending a pole at the show's opening. This is a young Carrie Ann Inaba, now better known as the longtime judge of *Dancing with the Stars*. She had gotten her US break in 1990 as part of the "Fly Girls" dance troupe on Fox's *In Living Color*, the primarily Black-cast alternative to NBC's *Saturday Night Live*. Briefly overlapping with Jennifer Lopez, Inaba has said of the troupe that she "felt so at home" with these "five multicultural girls [who] were going for their dreams and not afraid."[3] Prior to that, and after winning a talent show as an eighteen-year-old in Hawaii, Inaba was a popular singer in Japan, where, in addition to China and Ireland, she traces her ancestry. Her featured role in Madonna's concert came on the condition that she shave her head. Inaba only briefly hesitated. "But I was like, 'Are you kidding me? This is Madonna!'"

Inaba was also one of the Japanese twins, in Sailor Moon Garb, who had wanted to sleep with Austin Powers in the

[3]Monica Rizzo, "Dancing with the Stars' Carrie Ann Inaba," *People Magazine* (October 16, 2006).

2002 *Goldmember* movie, also starring Beyoncé as Foxxy Cleopatra, which had been all the rage with pubescent teenage boys at a time when I was a pubescent teenage boy. In that movie, Inaba's name was Fook Yu; her twin was Fook Mi. This was the twenty-first-century update to Papillon Soo Soo, who plays a sex worker in US-besieged Vietnam in Stanley Kubrick's *Full Metal Jacket*, before her famous words were taken up by 2 Live Crew in 1989: *Me so horny. Me love you long time.* Something ingrained in American culture usually casts the Asian woman's seeming phonetic difficulties as somehow hypersexual, desperate to please the white soldier or spy. As I also know as an Asian American gay man, this toggle can quickly turn Asians asexual, outside the thinkable of sexual objecthood. The phrase that would take off on gay dating apps the following decade was "no fats, no femmes, no Asians."

What an Asian American fan like me might therefore find so captivating about Inaba sliding down the poll, topless, alone, to open *The Girlie Show*—therefore to seem to be, for a moment, the title character of the show—was the simultaneous centrality and sexiness of her entrance, how she was sexy on her own, not as the object of someone else's gaze on the stage, even if that sexiness came at a cost, even if there is always a compromise to representation. Here, the compromise might also be what makes Inaba so beautifully queer in her role: the androgyny of this sexuality—the buzzed hair atop the exposed breasts. "Is she a boy or a girl?," one might wonder, if only aware of those two options. In their first book, *Gender Trouble*—published in 1990 and often considered a watershed moment in what has come to be called "queer theory" in higher education—the philosopher Judith Butler noted that when we ask of a newborn, "Is it a boy or a girl?" we are dealing with nothing less than what it means to be human.[4] A baby goes from being an ungendered "it," a mere thing, to being human by being assigned one of two gendered subject positions, boy or girl, he or she. Before "queer" became an identity category later, "queer theory" referred to efforts to explain how this kind of situation had been set up and what falls outside its normative assumptions—what kinds of people, community, desires, sex acts, and bodies can disrupt the assumption that everyone is cisgendered, straight, and destined for marriage and the production of more babies. What many of these theorists have pointed out is how race complicates what gets counted outside the normal, including who gets classified as "androgynous" whether or not they identify that way.

We tend to think of queerness as an attribute of individuals, a reference to the shape of their desire and the objects it takes. It is a shorthand for a kind of identity, whether sexual orientation or gender performance. But if we think of queerness more generally as a distance from a culture's norms of kinship, sex, and sexuality, many are considered queer not by choice or as an expression of their interior identities but through a violent expulsion from the central institutions by which a society imagines its reproduction and futurity, including marriage and the

---

[4]Judith Butler, *Gender Trouble: Feminism and the Subversion of Identity*, 2nd ed. (New York: Routledge, 2006), 151.

nuclear family. In this light, queerness may be a matter of racial as much as sexual difference or more precisely names the place where race and sexuality meet in the power games of our social construction of normativity and the material benefits that accompany it. At its most pathologizing, we have something like Daniel Patrick Moynihan's notoriously racist 1965 report, as Assistant Secretary of Labor under President Lyndon B. Johnson, that poverty in Black communities was an effect, rather than cause, of non-normative family structures, in particular the high number of single-mother households. At its most politically optimistic and transformative, we have the Black political theorist Cathy Cohen's assessment, in a classic 1997 essay titled "Punks, Bulldaggers, and Welfare Queens," that a coalition of those estranged from the white-nuclear-family-with-a-white-picket-fence ideal, including the seemingly straight figures listed in her title, might provide a powerful form of resistance.[5]

But this is not really the politics Madonna offers in *Erotica* or the concert video that accompanied it. What Madonna more often offers as a racial politics is the color-blind liberalism that, as she puts it in "Vogue," *it makes no difference if you're black or white.* In reality, it only makes no difference if you think race can be unloaded of accumulated histories

[5]Cathy J. Cohen, "Punks, Bulldaggers, and Welfare Queens: The Radical Potential of Queer Politics?," *GLQ: A Journal of Lesbian and Gay Studies* 3, no. 4 (1997): 437–65. See also Cathy Cohen, "The Radical Potential of Queer? Twenty Years Later," *GLQ: A Journal of Lesbian and Gay Studies* 25, no. 1 (2019): 140–4.

of dispossession and violence so as to become nothing more than striking a pose on the dance floor. The previous year, Michael Jackson had released a single with a nearly identical sentence (*it don't matter if you're black or white*) but with an additional awareness of violence on multiple scales, as rapped by cowriter Bill Bottrell: *It's a turf war on a global scale*. Without this awareness of violence, Madonna might be accused of reducing systemic racism to dance moves. And yet I would be lying to say I have not loved this and other songs, loved perhaps because of, not in spite of, the way the rhythm is always more progressive than the politics. I look at that color-blind vision and Madonna's multiracial crew of dancers in the same cosmopolitan uniform, and I sometimes see myself represented by my lack of representation, see myself on stage through being absent from it in any culturally specific way.

It's a similar form of oblique identification that draws many gay men to someone like Madonna in the first place, someone who, like Cher or Judy Garland, is neither gay nor a man (but may have dated or even, in the case of Garland, married one). When, as a high schooler, she had asked Christopher Flynn, the dance instructor she later memorialized in "In This Life," why gay guys liked Garland so much—or Marilyn Monroe, on whom Madonna would model so much of her public appearance, culminating in dating a Kennedy while running *The Blond Ambition* tour in 1990—Flynn responded, "I think it's because they're so tragic. I think that's what it is. You see them and you want to slit your wrists. Every gay man has wanted to slit his wrist at one time or another." At the time, Madonna thought, "If it takes being tragic to have gay friends, forget it."[6] But in the first decade of her recording career, she did cultivate gay friendships and especially a gay fan base, bonded not by the dry categories of demographics—age, sex, gender, sexuality—but by something more atmospheric, like being tragic had been for Garland. For Madonna, it was being a spectacle. And part of her spectacle has always been to offer queerness as some color-blind utopia, a place where her Black, Latinx, and Asian dancers all participate equally in the on-stage orgy.

In the chapters to follow, I look at several aspects of *Erotica* in the context of the 1990s. What the album did was, like wrapping up sex in the sentimental, resolve a number of tensions, always making Madonna both too old and too naive, both out of date and avant-garde, both an icon and a fossil—and either way belonging in a museum, worthy of admiration, preservation, and study. She is a Madonna, but also a whore—which means a businesswoman. She is white, but also, somehow, ethnically ambiguous—a global superstar claimed by Japan as much as England or the United States. She is dance, but also pop. Subcultural, but mainstream. A recurring theme throughout these many contradictions, however, is how racialization intersects with or complicates these binary axes of categories. Race divides the white gay cosmopolitan who summers in Paris and winters in Puerto Vallarta from the Black and brown underground who invented the dance moves they perform there, most famously the "Vogue" dance from the New York Harlem queer scene

[6]J. Randy Taraborrelli, *Madonna: An Intimate Biography of an Icon at Sixty* (London: Pan Books, 2019), 32–3.

that gave Madonna's most popular song its title. It's race that divides the single mother who is praised for being empowered and "having it all," an image of female independence, from the single mother who is pathologized as dependent, as a "welfare queen." Race comes between who gets to come out as queer, because they were presumed straight, and who was read, stereotyped, as queer before they knew it.

This book about Madonna's 1992 album is thus also a book about what she symbolizes, advances, or slows down in larger cultural transformations around race, gender, and sexuality, particularly in the United States. This is a book about how music tries to find a rhythm for the erotic in the context of rising conservatism, family values, and the devastation of the AIDS epidemic. It is a book about how mainstream pop relates to subcultures and profits off of them while also giving sometimes welcome exposure and resources to keep the subculture going. And it is about how the many roles Madonna plays—as "mother" to her dancers, as entertainer to the world, as a businesswoman to *Forbes*—also tell us about the many roles we play in our own lives and the challenge of integrating those roles or adopting an identity amid polarization and destabilization in our society.

* * *

To get at these questions, this book approaches *Erotica* not only historically, situating it within the political and social crises of its day, but also theoretically, drawing upon work in critical studies of gender, race, and sexuality. Madonna's rising career, and the inflection point marked by the 1992 release of this particular album, has been intimately connected with new work in academia. The year *Erotica* came out was the same year that the first book-length collection of academic essays on Madonna, titled *The Madonna Connection*, also appeared in the public sphere. In her introduction to the volume, editor Cathy Schwichtenberg recalls being named on an *Inside Edition* television episode that ran a "particularly nasty exposé about 'Madonna scholars.'"[7] Classes at college universities devoted to Madonna seemed, to the mainstream press, too frivolous, another benchmark from which to judge how far some culture warriors had gone in throwing out the canon of fine music, art, and literature. But it was Madonna who also helped new fields in academia grow and refine, because of the unique combination of styles, histories, and identities made by her music.

In particular, two academic fields of study were at important moments in their trajectory when Madonna became a central topic of conversation. The first is sometimes called cultural studies, definitively shaped by the Jamaican-born British theorist Stuart Hall. Cultural studies looks at how the domain of the "popular"—including pop culture, pop music—is where people make sense of their everyday lives. The popular can, then, be both a site of resistance and subversion, when people form countercultural interpretations that challenge the status quo of power through popular culture; or it can be pacifying and conservative, when pop

---

[7]Cathy Schwichtenberg, "Introduction," in *The Madonna Connection: Representational Politics, Subcultural Identities, and Cultural Theory*, ed. Cathy Schwichtenberg (Boulder, CO: Westview Press, 1993), 1.

music paints a limited sense of what is possible in life or in politics. In 1989, the professor John Fiske published two books that each centered in some way on Madonna: *Understanding Popular Culture* and *Reading the Popular*. What was important to Fiske was not to get stuck in the binary decisions over whether someone like Madonna was subversive or just entrenching status quo power relations. In part, this is because the economic and cultural nature of a work can diverge: something can economically make rich people, like Madonna, a lot of money, while still providing cultural resources, not to mention life-sustaining pleasure, for working-class movements and ideologies. As Fiske put it, "the fact that such pleasures serve the economic interests of the producers does not prevent them from serving the cultural interests of the consumers."[8]

The other academic field intimately connected with Madonna is what has come to be called queer theory, a transformation of gay and lesbian studies often symbolically tied to the 1990 publications of Judith Butler's *Gender Trouble* and Eve Kosofsky Sedgwick's *Epistemology of the Closet*. The first book, as I explore more in Chapter 2, is about the instability of gender, whereas the second book is about how gay/straight identification has been a central part of twentieth-century Western culture. Sexuality is polymorphous and has theoretically infinite dimensions of classification—from the type of activities people like, to the type of objects they do or do not like to incorporate into sex, to the types of roleplaying

[8]John Fiske, *Reading the Popular* (New York: Routledge, 1989), 118.

they do or not like, and so on—but ever since the nineteenth century, Western cultures have limited its definition to the gender of object choice (homosexual vs. heterosexual). One agenda for queer analysis could be to explain how this came to be and what its consequences are. Another agenda could be to see how communities of people as well as works of art and literature open up our concept of sexuality to be more expansive and less predictable.

Madonna has been important for this agenda because of her historical imagination—drawn constantly to Marlene Dietrich, for instance—and the way her performances do or do not expand our sense of sexuality. She has also been important because of her simple status as an icon, sometimes ambivalently, in different queer communities. For instance, writing the year before *Erotica* was released, *Village Voice* columnist Michael Musto discussed his own ambivalent relation as a gay man to Madonna's music:

> She shimmers into our fag imagination, spreads her legs for our dyke approbation, grabs us by the pudenda and makes us face things we didn't think it was possible to learn from pop music. After an hour's private session with her, we're aroused but wearing condoms, mad at her for ripping us off, somehow thanking her for noticing us, legitimizing us, pulling us by our bootstraps up out of hiding and into the public pleasuredome of scrutiny and success. . . . Deliriously, we imagine we're sitting *with* her in the arena—not cheering from the bleachers, but laughing alongside her onstage and sharing in the kudos from the throngs who recognize that we're a big part of

her triumph—even if any real attempt to get near our lady of the poses would have a bouncer dragging us out by the neck as she sang "keep people together" with her usual twisted sense of irony.[9]

Lisa Henderson, after quoting Musto in her contribution to *The Madonna Connection* collection, concludes with a note about ambivalence and contradiction that guides much of my own present book, and also brings together the fields of queer theory and popular culture studies:

> it is still too much to expect of a pop star that she resolve contradictions not of her own making (or even those that are), and it is unreasonable as well to think that in our fandom or in our critiques we will resolve in Madonna the contradictions that attract us in the first place. . . . But with vigilance, her work can be articulated to our struggles and our pleasures, offering us a place to play out both construct and essence and to do so, critically, on the captivating and thus politically powerful ground of the popular.[10]

In the following chapters, I, too, consider the "contradictions that attract us in the first place" to Madonna. Each chapter is

[9]Quoted in Lisa Henderson, "Justify Our Love: Madonna and the Politics of Queer Sex," in *The Madonna Connection: Representational Politics, Subcultural Identities, and Cultural Theory*, ed. Cathy Schwichtenberg (Boulder, CO: Westview Press, 1993), 122.

[10]Ibid., 124.

about one particular contradiction and how *Erotica* does or does not play out its tensions.

First, I turn to *Sex/Erotica*. Although the names for her two controversial products in 1992—the pornographic book and the studio album—they also name two different relations to sex, sexuality, and romance, particularly in the context of the HIV/AIDS epidemic. *Erotica* is less pornographic because it is interested in what I call "safe sex," sex that feels less dangerous not just physically but emotionally. In particular, I look at the resonances between the lyrics of key tracks on the album and contemporary queer poetry that mourns or ruminates over the people and community murdered by AIDS.

Second, in Chapter 2, I turn to subculture/mass culture to explore questions of appropriation in Madonna's music, particularly her relation to the cultural production of queer communities and communities of color. Here, I address debates over Madonna's appropriation of dance practices from the queer underground of Harlem's ball culture. What is at stake in many of these appropriations, I show, is not just the relation of a white woman to Black and brown queens but also the relation between the music industry and politics, where the seriousness of politics is sometimes used to legitimize the "popular" nature of mainstream cultural production. I situate Madonna's work in the culture wars of the early 1990s, in particular her seeming desire to be part of the controversies around the National Endowment for the Arts' funding of queer artists including Robert Mapplethorpe. I conclude with a close listening of key moments in which *Erotica* appropriates or even plagiarizes music from other traditions, in order to show how appropriation is often, for Madonna, about trying to keep a mood of erotic exoticism going.

Finally, in Chapter 3, I look at the contradiction between Madonna/whore, in particular how Madonna's status as a businesswoman is implicated in all the other tensions explored in the book as well. *Erotica* and *Sex* were the first releases of Madonna's new record label, Maverick, as part of a huge $50-million deal with Time Warner. I look at Madonna's self-stylizations as a businesswoman but especially as a sex worker, someone who sells sex. I'm interested in the allure of sex work to her and in particular what sex work represents in the popular imagination, especially in the context of a globalized free market. For many, sex work as the "oldest profession" has meant it is often on the cutting edge of work itself: how people labor, when, and in what ways. *Erotica* is aware of this, and it allegorizes all work as a kind of hustle.

Throughout these chapters, I draw upon my own experiences as a gay Asian American, who has both loved and, not hated, been frustrated by Madonna. But I also try to decenter cis male gayness as the end-all and be-all of queerness, not least because many of the dancers who originated vogueing in the New York ball scene would not have identified as gay but as trans or gender non-conforming. A more expansive notion of queerness, one attuned as much to gender identity as sexual orientation, is what teases out the ambivalences at the core of Madonna's sex/erotic, mainstream/subcultural, and virgin/whore contradictions.

1
Sex/Erotica

Truth or Dare, the intimate documentary following Madonna on her *Blond Ambition* tour in 1990, opens in a hotel room as the singer cleans up champagne bottles from the night before. The tour has just ended, and she's telling us about how the dancers and backup singers and musicians with her are in their feels about it. Madonna herself, she explains, is not:

> I didn't feel emotional because it was like it already ended for me. It's like when you know someone's dying . . . you have to make your peace before they die. I've done this with close friends of mine. I make my peace with it before it happens, so I don't get really hurt. And then when it happens it's like . . . I don't feel anything.

Madonna is not unfamiliar with death. Famously, her mother and namesake passed when she was five years old, and she has over the course of her life built up the defense mechanism she talks about here, a pre-mourning that makes the actual mourning less severe—like a vaccine. But the "close friends" she is talking about, in the plural, also allude to how frequently she has had to take the vaccine in recent years. *Erotica*'s "In This Life," as mentioned in the previous chapter, is about two friends who had died of AIDS. In the final US stop on the *Blond Ambition* tour, we see in footage on *Truth or Dare*, Madonna dedicated her performance to Keith Haring, the pop artist who had also recently died of AIDS. One of his final works, in support of the AIDS Coalition to Unleash Power, or ACT UP, showed three cartoon figures hearing no evil, seeing no evil, speaking no evil, under the slogan IGNORANCE = FEAR and above the slogan SILENCE = DEATH.

Madonna, for her part, had been speaking out against the culture of silence around HIV/AIDS since the mid-1980s. It was sometimes a difficult balance, to speak out while also entertaining, to rally while also mourning, or, in her case, pre-mourning so death never came as a terrible surprise. In a 1987 benefit at the Madison Square Garden, she told her audience, "I don't want to turn this into a morbid affair, but AIDS is a painful and mysterious disease that continues to elude us."[1] What ultimately made her a good spokeswoman, when she was one, was the impersonality she admitted in the *Truth or Dare* documentary. Madonna could be intensely personal at times, particularly in the context of her strained intimate relationships with men—her father, her husbands— although she did often find a way to make her life a spectacle rather than a quiet confession, one other strategy of not becoming too vulnerable. But in the context of HIV/AIDS,

[1]Vince Aletti, "Madonna: Madison Square Garden," *Rolling Stone*, no. 507 (August 27, 1987).

she did not have to identify as a survivor to be an advocate for survivors, and she did not resort to spectacle. Impersonality, in this context, became a resource. It meant Madonna did not have to have HIV to be in the fight against it. It meant she could talk about the issues, rather than about herself. Upon receiving an award from the American Foundation for AIDS Research, Madonna had to come out as being HIV negative, explaining that if she were positive, "I would be more afraid of how society would treat me for having the disease than the actual disease itself. If this is what I have to deal with for my involvement in fighting this epidemic, then so be it."[2]

It was in this way, too, that her lyrics which were not about her soul could also become loaded with meanings that spoke to new and different political contexts she could not have planned. In particular, there has always been a profound if surprising connection between dance music and mourning. The last poem from D. A. Powell's *Cocktails*, the final volume in his AIDS-inspired renovation of Dante's *Divine Comedy*, is called a "coda & discography." The poet enters a "queer niteclub," which entails stepping over the places haunted by queer deaths and murders—"missing. beaten. Died at the end of a prolonged illness"—in order to reach "the door marked HEAVEN." In this club, the dead are "reclaimed": "voyeurs, passion flowers, trolls, twinks, dancers, cruisers, lovers without lovers."[3] HEAVEN is a popular name of gay nightclubs, including the now-closed three-floor dance spot

[2]Ibid.

[3]D. A. Powell, *Cocktails: Poems* (Minneapolis, MN: Graywolf Press, 2004), 65.

in New York's Chelsea gayborhood or the still-open two-story dance spot in London. In the popular vernacular, the name means, as Powell suggests in the subtitle to his poem, "paradise." But what Powell's poem brings out is a more bittersweet, a darker, sense of the word: after all, to get to heaven, you have to die.

The music and poetry of sex often invoke heaven: his dick was like heaven; their body was heavenly. And when what is supposed to be the opposite is invoked, the meaning is the same: the sex was hot as hell. But whether we're in heaven or in hell, we're in an afterlife, which is to say after life. And in the context of an incurable sexually transmitted disease that was felt by many, at first, to be a death sentence, heaven and hell take on a heavier meaning.

The "discography" in Powell's poem is a list of the dance floor tracks that might be playing in HEAVEN, songs that take on new, haunting meanings in the context of AIDS, including Gloria Gaynor's "I Will Survive," Vivien Vee's "Blue Disease," Ashford and Simpson's "Found a Cure," Carol Douglas's "Doctor's Orders," and finally Sylvester's "Stars." He doesn't mention Madonna—she's not in the disco genre he's plumbing—but her discography, too, consistently makes the sex/death/heaven connection, going back to the first track on her eponymous first album, "Lucky Star": *Shine your heavenly body tonight.* A quick sampling of other heavenly moments, à la Powell:

Oooh, you're an angel. ("Angel")

I hear your voice, it's like an angel sighing . . .
Heaven help me ("Like a Prayer")

Whether it's heaven or hell
I'm gonna be living to tell ("Survival")

She's got herself a little piece of heaven
Waiting for the time when Earth shall be as one ("Ray of
   Light")

Bring the heaven and the stars
Down to Earth for me ("Isaac")

But the best line of physical intimacy on the brink of the afterlife comes from the chorus of *Erotica*'s "Deeper and Deeper": *I can't help falling in love . . . Kisses sent from heaven above.* The trope of losing control of one's self in the face of love becomes erotic, but only chastely with kisses. And yet their source in heaven suggests a kind of connection across heaven and earth. It's like God giving life to Adam in Michelangelo's fresco on the ceiling of the Sistine Chapel, although not a finger touch but a kiss. Madonna's song brings out the eroticism hidden, or not so hidden, within religious iconography: nude Adam touched by another man, his God. Even the most controversial appropriation of religious imagery—Christ's crucifixion—has served homoerotic interests in the history of its visual representation, just like the story of another martyr, Saint Sebastian, pierced by arrows, has been seen as a penetrated twink. Christ's body is after all on display in his underwear.

   This is one reason dance music might be the soundtrack for the AIDS epidemic, not just because of its associations with the disco floors on which gay men congregated but because of its lyrical linking of mourning and horniness. In

April of the year *Erotica* was released, *Rolling Stone* covered a tribute to Freddie Mercury, the rock star who had died the previous year of complications from AIDS. The article singles out Madonna, "whose activism has outclassed that of any other pop star" and who "continues to contribute time and money toward the fight against AIDS."[4] Unlike Madonna, Mercury was reluctant to discuss AIDS until his death was imminent. Why? Although the most important answer might be that Madonna had the luxury of turning on and off attention to AIDS, unlike Mercury who was chronically living with it, *Rolling Stone* offers a theory dealing instead with the genre split between rock and pop, and certainly rock and dance music:

> Every day we hear of new AIDS casualties from other areas of the arts. A generation of talent from theater, dance, classical music, film and the fine arts has already been decimated. Why not rock & roll? Has anyone fooled himself into believing that rock & roll junkies never shared syringes and metalhead studs never shared groupies? Are rockers too macho to admit that they could be susceptible to a disease that many associate with homosexuality?

In contrast, Madonna's music world seems primed to provide space for AIDS activism—because her music is not just about her but about the dance floor. The singer who would write an album called *Confessions on a Dance Floor* always linked the personal ("confessions") with a collective space

[4]Steve Hochman and Mary Herczog, "AIDS and Rock: Sound of Silence," *Rolling Stone*, no. 629 (April 30, 1992).

("a dance floor"). These are not rock songs that glamorize death in the form of the overdose. These are dance tracks that acknowledge the deathliness of sex and also the heavenliness of sex—and the mourning that must be done for those who are *in heaven above.*

*   *   *

Let me tell you about the most unusual place I've heard "Deeper and Deeper" played or at least a remix of it. It was in the Steamworks Baths in Chicago.

Though they vary in their extravagance and the baroqueness of their architecture (gloryhole mazes!), most gay bathhouses are pretty similar. Usually, there's *some* sort of "bath" to warrant the name: a public sauna or steam room or pool where naked men or men in tiny towels might start checking each other out. There are usually dimly lit hallways with bedrooms—literally: rooms that are just large enough to hold a twin bed—where some of these men will couple or throuple. There will be more public venues for hooking up, too, the dungeons with slings and, again, the mazes with gloryholes. But there will always be spaces that don't scream sex. Somewhere there's a gym, which is a great place to cruise, sure, but not only. If you're in Europe, there's probably a bar and lounge. But wherever you are, there will always be a screen somewhere playing music videos. There will be screens playing porn, too, and of course there are a lot of dicks and asses. But when it comes to the screens with music videos, what's on play are usually remixes of songs by the great divas: Cher, Janet Jackson, and of course Madonna.

Bette Midler says she got her start in the gay bathhouses of the late 1960s and early 1970s. Her debut album, *The Divine Miss M*, is named after a personality Midler created for the Continental Baths crowd in New York. The album is composed largely of covers of songs drawn from too many different social and regional contexts to form a coherent whole: from the Black R&B of Bobby Freeman's "Do You Want to Dance," through the Southern girl-pop of "Chapel of Love" originally made famous by the Dixie Cups, and up to the rockabilly "Delta Dawn" and the jump blues of "Boogie Woogie Bugle Boy." There's a kind of utopianism to this eclecticism: everyone's welcome. But the going from one song to another in *The Divine Miss M* is also like emotional whiplash. Immediately following the snappy rendition of "Chapel of Love" (*We're going to the chapel and we're gonna get mar-ar-ar-ied*) is an understated cover of "Superstar" that suggests the marriage has already disintegrated (*Don't you remember, you told me you loved me baby?*). "Daytime Hustler," with its 1970s pimp vibe, is followed up by "Am I Blue?," which opens with a moody, plodding piano solo.

I thought about *Divine Miss M* when I recently experienced an emotional whiplash of my own at the Steamworks Baths in Chicago where Madonna's "Deeper and Deeper" was on the screen. The opening lyrics are *I can't help falling in love*, and I probably don't have to tell you that *deeper and deeper* refers to the depths of this fall, a drowning in love, rather than a dirty plea to a lover. The song opens with synthetic, angelic chords suspended long enough that you can get inside their sound, mimicking that sense of drowning, of being out of touch with the world because so fully immersed in something else, and even the remix playing at Steamworks, which leaned more into the repetitious bass beat that comes later, still offered that atmospheric sense. In this space, some of the lyrics take on a different meaning. *Daddy couldn't be all wrong* hits different when there's a leather daddy in the corner checking you out. And in this space, the refrain—*I can't help falling in love*—sounds more like a warning. You don't come to a bathhouse to fall in love. You don't come here looking to get *mar-ar-ar-ied.*

Or, in some perverse way, do you? The naked boys who sat cross-legged before the emerging diva at the Continental Baths in the 1970s did not seem to find "Chapel of Love" incompatible with whatever they did in the backrooms. Maybe, on some nights, they even came to the Baths more for Midler's performance, which was after all guaranteed, than for finding Mr. Right Now, which was not. Maybe what is so erotic about sound, rather than pornographic vision, is that atmospheric sense of going deeper and deeper, how it charges a space in a way that everyone is experiencing in the same way. Maybe no two people are looking at the same thing or the same person—we all have our own type—but the soundtrack means everyone is listening to the same thing. There's an eroticism to feeling your body hit by the same invisible but still visceral soundwaves as everyone else in the same room. There's a connection which, strictly speaking, isn't sexual or at least genital. But it's there, and, like all soundtracks, it might even be doing the heavy lifting of setting the mood when the plot isn't very exciting.

Sound provides another connection, too, which is to a different time. A song comes on and we might be reminded of all the different times and places we've heard it played before. Although remixed, the distinctly 1990s disco feel of "Deeper and Deeper" still comes through in its synth bass notes held for long durations for strings to dance on top of. In the original album version, there's an attempt at a fast beat, which carries the song but becomes just a little boring the longer the song goes: it's one of the danciest of the album's songs, but it's also one of its longest. You can imagine a DJ in the 1990s giving it a little twirl before skipping to something else. But in the early 1990s, you couldn't hear Madonna in a bathhouse. Not because she wasn't already a gay icon, which of course she was. But because there weren't bathhouses.

In 1984, when some people still might have referred to AIDS by its original name, GRID, short for Gay-Related Immune Deficiency, San Francisco—that gay mecca and therefore that ground zero for an epidemic that devastated the gay community—shut down its bathhouses. Well, technically, the city said bathhouses could stay open if the staff became voyeur spies, removing all bedroom doors so patrons could be under constant surveillance to make sure they weren't having condomless sex. The bathhouses closed. It wasn't until February 2020 that legislation was introduced at the San Francisco Board of Supervisors to remove these restrictions and re-allow private rooms. The timing was unfortunate: a month later *everything* would be closed in San Francisco due to a new pandemic, Covid-19.

In 1987, the gay cultural critic Douglas Crimp wrote an essay called "How to Have Promiscuity in an Epidemic." The government had pretty much failed to do anything to help those who were suffering the most from AIDS at the time, except for criminalizing them. The year 1987, five years after "AIDS" was first named, was the first year President Reagan managed to even say the word in public. But gays had learned to care for themselves, Crimp thought, for instance, developing caregiving networks that fostered a kind of intimacy unseen before, often with strangers caring for strangers because they were bonded by a common identity rather than biological relation. Most importantly, Crimp thought that whereas someone like San Francisco City thought the answer to a sexually transmitted disease was to shut down sex, gays had found ways to transform sex. He lauded

> the achievements of a sexual community whose theory and practice of sex made it possible to meet the epidemic's most urgent requirement: the development of safe sex practices. . . . We were able to invent safe sex because we have always known that sex is not, in an epidemic or not, limited to penetrative sex. Our promiscuity taught us many things, not only about the pleasures of sex, but about the great multiplicity of those pleasures. It is that psychic preparation, that experimentation, that conscious work on our own sexualities that has allowed many of us to change our sexual behaviors.[5]

Safe sex. I think we think we know what these words mean. But I don't think Crimp has that meaning in mind. It's not that gay men invented condoms and dental dams.

---

[5]Douglas Crimp, "How to Have Promiscuity in an Epidemic," *October*, no. 43 (1987): 253.

It's that they invented a whole new set of sexual acts and touches that didn't need condoms and dental dams. Michel Foucault, the French philosopher who had begun writing a multivolume *History of Sexuality* before he died of AIDS in 1984, liked to say that the only sexual practice invented in the twentieth century was the fisting he saw (and really enjoyed) in bathhouses, and that may be one of the things Crimp is talking about.[6] Fisting someone's butt can't transmit HIV (unless the fister's hand is bleeding). But when he talks about the "great multiplicity" of pleasures, Crimp means finding something erotic throughout the body, not limited to what we think of as the sexual organs. It means kinds of nonsexual touch and contact that provide a sexual thrill. Thirty years later, when Christian Grey runs a feather along the back of Anastasia Steele in the mommy porn *Fifty Shades* series or slaps a paddle against her thigh, some of these kinds of touch don't seem that radical anymore. But even these expand what we might think of as what the erotic contains, makes the erotic overflow from the boundaries mapped out in anatomical charts.

Enter the bathing sound of "Deeper and Deeper" into the bathhouse. The lyrics are about love, about heartbreak, about the lessons in romance *my mama told me*, all of which seem out of place in a sex dungeon. But the rhythm is sexual, somehow, in the "multiplicity of pleasures" sense of the sexual—the syncopation like two bodies coming in and out of sync, joining and unfurling. Further into the song,

[6]See David M. Halperin, *Saint Foucault: Towards a Gay Hagiography* (New York: Oxford University Press, 1997), 92.

Madonna borrows a line from her earlier "Vogue": *Let your body move to the music.*

This form of instruction is what makes *Erotica*'s politics of sex different from that of the pornographic coffee table book *Sex*. On the first page of *Sex*, Madonna explained that she does "not condone unsafe sex," but she "rarely thinks of condoms" when she fantasizes about sex, because "my fantasies take place in a perfect world, a place without AIDS." In fact, half of this first page—which is all text, in all caps—goes on about condoms and how they "are not only necessary but mandatory": "If I were to make my dreams real, I would certainly use condoms. Safe sex saves lives. Pass it on." This split between dream and reality, between hot bareback sex in the imagination and the "mandatory" sex with condoms in practice, is the conventional safe sex education stance, a moralistic one that says condoms are a sacrifice but one we must make for the greater good, a cross to bear. A different strategy might have been to eroticize the limit, to invest in a fantasy that made condoms sexy: not necessary but hot, not mandatory but desired—like fetish gear. The difference is between an education that tells you what not to do, an education of rules, and an education that makes you want to do something, an education of positive reinforcement. "Deeper and Deeper"'s borrowing from "Vogue"— *Let your body move to the music*—is a positive education, an invitation to safer sex rather than a schoolmarm lecturing you about condoms.

Madonna's other atmospheric song on *Erotica*—the other song that invites an audience to drown in the sound and relishes in the water metaphors to go with it—is "Rain," which is also the album's most melodious track. Like "Deeper and Deeper," the track is introduced with strings that open up into an expansive tableau, somewhat eerily modified by a hi-hat which is probably supposed to sound like light thunder in the distance. The sound is not unlike the similarly dreamy and similarly stringy opening of Enya's similarly watery "Caribbean Blue" released the previous year. But as Madonna's voice enters into and elevates the arrangement, she takes it in a new direction. The song begins with tactile lyrics: *I feel it. It's coming. Rain, feel it on my fingertips. Hear it on my window pane. Your love's coming down like rain.*

Let's move past the knee-jerk reaction to sneer a bit at another weather metaphor to talk about love. We're also going to have to ignore a bit later on in the song when she cheers about the sun coming out. She can't have it both ways: either love is rain or love is the sun. What matters here is this invitation to *feel* and a feeling that is not really an emotion at first, not the love itself but a physical sensation, a tingling of the fingertips. In the original music video, when Madonna holds the first "Rain" note, her face is blurred in the background and what we see in the foreground, lightly caressing the microphone, are her fingertips. This is some safe sex. It's sex in the tingling of fingertips, sex that draws attention to the details of the body. But it's also solo sex. Because like so many songs in *Erotica*, this is Madonna singing alone, at a distance from the lover she addresses— *waiting for all the dark clouds bursting in a perfect sky.* If this is erotic, it's also sad, or sadness as a kind of erotica: something that is simultaneously all-encompassing emotionally and particularly physical.

The same year Madonna released *Erotica*, the gay poet Thom Gunn released a book of elegiac poetry, *The Man with Night Sweats*, titled after a common symptom of AIDS. The first poem of the book is called "The Hug." This is a poem, like "Rain," addressed to a distant lover, a lost lover. The speaker remembers a simple moment of physical intimacy from their past together, a hug after a boozy birthday dinner. The description of this physical intimacy takes up most of the poem—the exact ways in which the two bodies came together in an embrace, down to an almost clinical choreography:

> Your instep to my heel,
> My shoulder-blades to your chest.
> It was not sex, but I could feel
> The whole strength of your body set,
> Or braced, to mine.[7]

But this intimacy, we are told outright, is explicitly "not sex." Or, in the words of Douglas Crimp, this is "safe sex": an erotic connection but one that could not transmit HIV, an "experimentation" in sexual contact without sexual organs. In a PhD dissertation, "The AIDS Poets, 1985-1995: From Anti-Elegy to Lyric Queerness," Aaron Bradley Gorelick also calls this Gunn's "ambivalence over touch's implications amidst the crisis": drawn to physical contact but phobic of that contact's vector as a transmission of disease.[8]

---

[7]Thom Gunn, *The Man with Night Sweats: Poems* (New York: Farrar, Straus and Giroux, 1992), 3.

[8]Aaron Bradley Gorelick, "The AIDS Poets, 1985-1995: From Anti-Elegy to Lyric Queerness" (PhD diss., UCLA, 2014), 129.

Each of the lines in "The Hug" has at least one other line to rhyme with: snug and hug, chest and pressed. They belong together, fit inside each other in a union just like the speaker's *shoulder-blades against your chest*. Each of the lines has a rhyming partner, that is, except for one: toward the end, the speaker remembers his lover's body *braced to mine*. It's the saddest line in the poem. Because "mine," that first-person pronoun, is the one word that's left dangling at the end of a line without a companion to rhyme with somewhere else. "Mine" is all alone—and so, too, is the speaker of this "mine," the speaker whose lover is probably dead, leaving only the memory of what the speakers calls *your secure firm dry embrace*.

This is a love, like Madonna's, that you feel in your fingertips. It's an eroticism that doesn't get you hard or wet (*dry embrace* is, on the face of it, probably the least sexy kind of embrace) but is almost more erotic because of it, because there isn't an easy way to release it. It's an eroticism intensified by loneliness, by loss, an eroticism that cannot be consummated.

When Madonna performed "Rain" in *The Girlie Show* the following year (the only time she performed it on a tour), its function as a kind of mood killer, a de-escalation of interpersonal sex, was confirmed by its placement in the setlist: it closes Act 1, the "Dominatrix" act, and it does so by sentimentalizing whatever sexiness that act had originally promised. Madonna sits on a stool singing along with longtime backup singers Niki Haris and Donna LeRoy and then the unsexiness intensifies. First, it begins with the reappearance of a Pierrot, the stock mime figure whose overflowing white clothes and white makeup serve as a motif throughout the concert, helping to cool things down. Then, "Rain" inspires, perhaps predictably, a return to the 1952 Gene Kelly musical film *Singin' in the Rain*; as Madonna exits the stage to prepare for the next act, her male backup dancers take over, in full suits dancing with umbrellas.

My favorite parts of *Singin' in the Rain*, the movie, are when Kelly sits down in a chair and someone else dances for him. The scenes are so weird, Gene sitting while the others dance. Maybe they're just a way to keep Gene on stage for a number he's not a part of. But it's the fact that they're dancing for Gene that makes these scenes seem so great. I sometimes call them lap dances, and because the dancers are guys, I used to think these lap dances were very, very gay. It's kind of hard not to. If you've seen the way Frank Sinatra looks at Gene Kelly, whom he calls a "wolf," in *Anchors Aweigh*, you know what I mean. Yet it was also our patron saint of queer theory, Eve Kosofsky Sedgwick, who said a couple of years before *Erotica* that sometimes we're too quick to go looking for gay subtexts.[9] Writing about Henry James—by all other accounts America's best and also gayest novelist—Sedgwick said we were probably missing a lot of the complexity of sexuality by constantly unmasking the gayness of authors. What if the permanent bachelorhood of James's characters was less proof of a repressed homosexuality, Sedgwick wondered, and instead something much simpler? Whatever happened to your old-fashioned misanthrope, someone who just doesn't

---

[9]Eve Kosofsky Sedgwick, *Epistemology of the Closet* (Berkeley: University of California Press, 1990), chapter 5.

like other people? Some people just don't give a fuck. Some people are asexual.

Gene Kelly movies are undeniably homo*social*. It's kind of a joke sometimes: in *American in Paris*, Gene is dancing and singing accompanied by his male best friend and the lyrics require him to say "Grab your partner" even though there's no female partner in sight. But are the movies homo*sexual*? In *On the Town*, Gene and Frank Sinatra join forces again as sailors on leave, this time joined by Jules Munshin, a queeny third who gets dipped by his heterosexual love interest, a severe scientist. There's gender reversal, in other words, which is often code for gayness. But rewatching the film recently, I was struck by how it doesn't so much seem to be about the open secret of gayness but an idea of fun that isn't about desire at all. These guys aren't just dancing to dance around their sexuality. And not just because Hollywood censorship would bar it but because it's fun—and this seems important that all these movies are fun before they are anything else—to imagine dancing just to dance or imagining a relationship where fucking isn't the goal by which everything else is judged as a step toward. Sexuality is more often a narrative for us, something with a beginning, middle, and end. Something that escalates from kissing in a tree to a baby in a baby carriage, from first base to third base, from holding hands on the first date to all the expectations of the third.

What seems so perverse about these musicals—perverse in a good way—is how they slow down or outright reject that kind of narrative progress. Consider one of the lap dances in *Singin' in the Rain*. Gene's goofy best friend, played by

Donald O'Connor, sits his old boy down and entertains him with a series of antics designed to "Make 'Em Laugh." That's all that matters: laughter. This isn't a seduction. It's a pause in the narrative to enjoy some goofiness. The goofiness of these lap dances rejects some sexual regime in which you have an "object" (your partner) you want to possess and move through a series of steps together toward the finish line or home base. They don't offer some counternarrative, trading gayness for straightness. Instead, they ask us to give up narrative altogether.

This is how I interpret the nod to *Singin' in the Rain* in this final scene of Act I of *The Girlie Show*, this scene in which "Rain" announces there will be no girlie show in the traditional sense. It's offering, not sex but a world in which something like fun and laughter and dancing just to dance might be what you want, a world that was desperately wanted, by some, reeling from the AIDS epidemic. I don't want to give Madonna too much credit here. She is not the bard of AIDS. She is not the gay men who Douglas Crimp says invented safe sex or the gay men like Thom Gunn who put the mourning of a devastated community into rhyme. I repeat: "Deeper and Deeper" is too long! "Rain" says love is like rain but then love is like the sun and it's like words don't matter! But what I've been trying to figure out is why "Deeper and Deeper" is playing at a gay sex club at all.

Here's why I think it is: it's not just that the song captures something about the conjunction of sadness and eroticism, which was gay sex in the middle of a sexually transmitted pandemic. It's not just that its textured, immersive, atmospheric sound is erotic and its disco beat even a bit thrilling despite the best intentions of its lyrics to be almost militantly dull, constantly invoking a boner-chilling *mama*. It's also because of what both of these things add up to: safe sex. Sex that is safe *because* it reminds you of love but isn't love. Sex that is safe *because* it is something you feel in your fingertips instead of in your dick. Sex that is safe *because* it is a bit boring, because Mr. Right Now is less emotionally demanding than Mr. Right and because there are a dozen others just like him waiting in the steam room.

*　*　*

The gay cultural critic David Halperin has also wondered about love songs playing at bathhouses in a provocative essay titled "What Is Sex For?" Halperin's opening puzzle is occasioned by hearing a hit Adele single playing in two separate bathhouses; he then reflects on the "blatant dissonance" between lyric and space: "Why play 'Someone Like You' in a gay bathhouse? That is, why play this song—about broken hearts, romantic longing, and the search for love—in a setting that is designed not for people looking for love but for people looking for sex?"[10] I don't mean to substitute one essentialist account of the bathhouse for the other—to suggest that the bathhouse is *really* about entertainment and fun rather than "designed for people looking for sex"—but to draw attention to the multiplicity of activities and scenes of immersion the bathhouse affords. It matters that baths do have not only the cubicles in which

---

[10]David M. Halperin, "What Is Sex For?," *Critical Inquiry* 43, no. 1 (2016): 3.

Halperin waits for "someone whom I might want to touch, suck, fuck, fist, kiss, rim, whatever" but also gyms, theaters, dungeons, and, of course, *baths*: the whirlpool, the sauna, the steam room. The website for IDM, Halperin's "favorite" Parisian bathhouse, advertises, sprawling across its five floors, "multiples espaces, au gré de vos envies" and then provides a list under four separate categories: yes, *sex* (e.g., slings, themed cabins, and orgy beds), but also *sport* (weight rooms, cardio machines), *détente* (an extra-large hammam, TV shows), and *divers* (a bar, smoking lounge, and magazine stand).

In the bathhouse, Eve Kosofsky Sedgwick's eternally useful axiom, "people are different from each other," means in part that people go to the bathhouse for different reasons and may get different effects out of identical activities.[11] Some people, like apparently Halperin, go looking for sex, but even if that's your only goal, you're likely to spend a lot of time not fucking but cruising: walking around, lurking in spaces to see if someone new will finally come along. There can be a pleasure to the cruise as well as to erotic waiting that is distinct from the pleasures of sex. In addition to looking for sex, or as an alternative to it, some people go to watch; some people go to socialize; some people go for free HIV/STD testing; some people go to work out. Perhaps, for some, part of the appeal of the bathhouse is the feeling you could live your life surrounded by sex or that all the time you're not fucking at the bath is still defined in relation to the fucking you do or

---

[11]Sedgwick, *Epistemology of the Closet*, 22.

could have done. Outside the bath, spaces of in-between often seem defined by capitalism or by romance: one is between jobs, between marriages. In the bath, there may be the sense you could live your life and access the world's institutions between fucks: you could go to the hospital (get tested), go to the bar (more likely in European baths), go to the theater, or go to the gym in the space between sexual encounters.

This is one reason, I want to suggest, that *Erotica* is one of the most eclectic of Madonna's albums, like Midler's *Divine Miss M*. On the one hand, the range of genres *Erotica* entertains says something about the diversity of her audience, her desire to bring together people from across social positions and places. This sense of a mosaic also recalls the largest activist artistic intervention in the AIDS epidemic, the AIDS Memorial Quilt whose ongoing collection of panels since the 1980s is currently estimated to weigh over 50 tons. Each panel is a contribution memorializing the life of someone who has died of AIDS; the panels are 3 x 6 feet, the size of a grave. Because of the stigma attached to AIDS and the marginalized communities disproportionately affected by it, many biological families did not recognize the deaths of victims, and many funeral homes refused services to victims as well. Instead of privatizing death, the quilt made these deaths public, impossible to look away from, a particularly powerful statement when installed on October 11, 1987, on the National Mall in Washington, D.C., as part of the National March on Washington for Lesbian and Gay Rights. The quilt is both highly individual and highly communal, a dynamic that the poet Timothy Liu has brought out in his poem entitled "The Quilt," which begins:

These are my lovers

            whose patches of color fade,

whose stitches have run

            wild in their patterns

of grief: the men who die

            and die in each other's arms,

leaving us their names.[12]

Notice the movement the poem makes from "my lovers" to "leaving us their names": from the personal "I" to the collective "we." In this movement, Liu expresses the political nature of his elegy: not just the loss of a loved one but the loss of a community, a loss felt to the community. Celebrating individual life within collective catastrophe is one thing the quilt attempts to do, just as *Erotica* expresses a different milieu with each song's genre.

But in addition to summoning a community, the genre range of *Erotica* is also, like Douglas Crimp suggested in his essay on safe sex, a way of multiplying kinds of pleasure, just like a bathhouse has multiple institutions in one: gym, concert venue, spa. Take your pick, *Erotica* says. Pick your pleasure, even if it's not fucking. *Put your hands all over my body* is, notably, not talking about genitals.

---

[12]Timothy Liu, *Vox Angelica* (Cambridge, MA: Alice James Books, 1992), 56.

This, finally, is what distinguishes *Erotica* from *Sex*, and more generally, the erotic from the pornographic or even directly sexual. The gay cultural critic Leo Bersani's most influential essay, written during the height of the AIDS epidemic, begins with this memorable line: "There is a big secret about sex: most people don't like it."[13] He was talking about how a lot of people are afraid of the loss of control they experience when they have sex—literally, in the seconds of losing control of the body in orgasm, but also figuratively in the fact that in sex we encounter our own incoherence, the disorienting nature of our desires and needs and wants. For Bersani, this is what might actually be radical about sex. Rather than celebrate the utopianism of a sexual liberation politics that turns orgasms into butterflies and fairy dust, sex might be transgressive because of its ability to unmake us instead of define us. He thought this was particularly important for gay men, who by enjoying being fucked and finding orgasmic *jouissance* in it could also unmake their attachment to a toxic form of masculinity:

> If sexuality is socially dysfunctional in that it brings people together only to plunge them into a self-shattering and solipsistic jouissance that drives them apart, it could also be thought of as our primary hygienic practice of nonviolence. Gay men's "obsession" with sex, far from being denied, should be celebrated—not because of its communal virtues, not because of its subversive potential for parodies of machismo, not because it offers a model

---

[13]Leo Bersani, "Is the Rectum a Grave?," *October* 43 (1987): 197.

of genuine pluralism to a society that at once celebrates and punishes pluralism, but rather because it never stops re-presenting the internalized phallic male as an infinitely loved object of sacrifice.[14]

This seems to be the politics of *Sex*. It wants to lose identity through S&M and sex, thus Madonna's morphing into an alter ego dominatrix she calls Dita. But this is not the politics of *Erotica*, which does want something more nurturing, which wants to rebuild ego after the bruising losses of community members to AIDS and medical neglect.

Erotica departs not just from *Sex* but also from the cultural product that completed Madonna's trifecta of sexual controversy in the winter of 1992–3: the erotic thriller *Body of Evidence*, produced by Dino De Laurentis, who had turned to psychological horror movies in the 1980s after the earlier success of the *Godfather* movies. *Body of Evidence* wanted to be the success that *Fatal Attraction* had been in 1987, catapulted by Glenn Close's performance as a woman who becomes obsessed with Michael Douglas's married character after a weekend fling. That film was the highest grossing in 1987, and *Body of Evidence* had the star power to rival: Willem Dafoe as a lawyer married to Julianne Moore who becomes involved with Madonna, his client who is accused of murdering an older man she had seduced. Allegedly, she had coerced this man, who had a heart condition, into rougher and more intense BDSM until he finally died of a heart attack, leaving her $8 million in his will.

[14]Ibid., 222.

Body of Evidence foregrounds the deadliness of sex: it matters that it is sex itself that is the cause of death, rather than parasexual violence, like Madonna wielding a knife in a violent frenzy. At the opening remarks in her trial, the prosecutor played by Joe Montega says of Madonna's character: "she is not only the defendant—she is the murder weapon itself." He elaborates: "But can sex be called a weapon? Yes. And what a deadly weapon Rebecca Lawson [Madonna's character] made of it. . . . When this trial is over you will see her no differently than a gun, or a knife or any other instrument used as a weapon. She is a killer. And the worst kind—one who disguised herself as a loving partner." It is a telling accusation, in line with the Madonna/whore binary I'll explore at greater length in the final chapter: even more than murder, Madonna's real crime seems to have been faking affection.

Throughout the film, the murder victim is implicitly and then explicitly coded as gay. Early on, the detectives wonder if he ever used poppers during their sexual intercourse, since amyl nitrate is sometimes prescribed for people with a heart condition. This drug has strong associations with the gay community, where it can be used as an aphrodisiac and as a muscle relaxant, making receptive anal sex more comfortable. Later, Dafoe's character asks Madonna how she found others in the BDSM community, using language similar to that of coming out or finding people "like you": "When you first met Andrew, how did you know that he was like you?" Madonna's character answers: "I was at a party, and there was a huge crowd of people, but we just saw each other, and we knew." They are at a restaurant, and Madonna offers: "You want me to look around and tell you if someone here has the same taste that I do?" Here, BDSM becomes an allegory for talking about other sexual subcultures. Finally, in the climactic scene of being questioned on the stand, Madonna reveals that she had found the victim in bed with another man, which she took as a betrayal and reason to leave him the night he was killed, meaning she couldn't be the killer. Although we learn she is, of course, actually guilty, her testimony wins over the jury. The lesson seems to be clear: having sex with another man is just one kink too far, gayness is just too much to swallow. In this way, the dead man comes out as having been, in the popular imagination, dead already, or dying: a symptom of gayness.

BDSM in the cultural imagination addressed by *Body of Evidence* both stands in for and finally departs from a gay referent. It also becomes coded as a geographic and class matter more than a matter of sexuality. Early in the film, as detectives investigate the murder scene, they find nipple clamps and handcuffs. At first, only one detective recognizes the clamps for what they are. "How would you know?" another asks, to which someone explains: "He's from L.A." For his own part, he explains, "I just happen to be a well-informed individual." "This is kinky shit," someone concludes. The linking of kink with L.A., or perhaps more specifically Hollywood, as a matter of being "well-informed" suggests the extent to which kinky sex has been coded as something about cultural capital and open-mindedness. It is about being worldly, educated, and with some history of living in a big city. During the culture wars of the 1990s explored at greater length in the next chapter, this set of associations helped conservatives to counterpoise alternative sexualities and the "average American"—understood as white, without a college degree, and preferably from the Midwest.

But this set of associations is not shared by *Erotica*, which is more careful not to collapse the pornographic and alternative communities. This is not least because *Erotica* is not as pornographic as either *Sex* or *Body of Evidence*. The film features multiple prolonged scenes in which we see every inch of Madonna's body, especially in her apparently preferred position of riding either her murder victim or her lawyer in cowgirl. The pornographic nature of this is heightened by having us first see her having sex on a video: it seems her victim liked to make home movies with her (and other partners). The tape is still playing as police investigate the scene, drawing our attention to the sensationalism of images. In contrast, the music of *Erotica* is both less explicit and more sentimental than sensational. Madonna still performs as the dominatrix Dita in the album, but we certainly don't get nipple clamps, poppers, or nudity—not even an explicit inventory of genitals or body parts doing their thing.

In her influential essay "Uses of the Erotic: The Erotic as Power," the Black feminist writer Audre Lorde contrasts the erotic with the pornographic. The erotic, for Lorde, is a feeling rather than an action: it "is not a question only of what we do; it is question of how acutely and fully we can feel in the doing."[15] The erotic is being fully present in what one is

---

[15]Audre Lorde, *Sister Outsider: Essays and Speeches* (Trumansburg, NY: Crossing Press, 1984), 54.

doing, which means it is a spiritual experience that need not accompany any particular action, such as sex. In contrast, "pornography is a direct denial of the power of the erotic, for it represents the suppression of true feeling. Pornography emphasizes sensation without feeling."[16] Lorde thought getting in touch with this erotic component was particularly important for women, who had been taught by patriarchal societies to step outside of their own bodies and devote themselves to the care of others. "When I speak of the erotic, then, I speak of it as an assertion of the lifeforce of women; of that creative energy empowered, the knowledge and use of which we are now reclaiming in our language, or history, our dancing, our loving, our work, our lives."[17] Finding the erotic will lead women to demand different and better lives: "that deep and irreplaceable knowledge of my capacity for joy comes to demand from all of my life that it be lived within the knowledge that such satisfaction is possible, and does not have to be called *marriage,* nor *god,* nor *an afterlife.*"[18]

Lorde first presented her essay orally at the Fourth Berkshire Conference on the History of Women, at Mount Holyoke College, in 1978. The scene matters: it's communal. She's talking to other women in a room of women, suggesting the ways in which the erotic is linked to the group instead of the individual—not to a sexual partner but to an activist community. "To share the power of each other's feeling is

[16]Ibid.
[17]Ibid., 55.
[18]Ibid., 57.

different from using another's feelings as we would use a kleenex. When we look the other way from our experience, erotic or otherwise, we use rather than share the feelings of those others who participate in the experience with us. And use without consent of the used is abuse."[19] The kleenex metaphor is particularly important: a mass-produced product brand-named until it became generic, meant for disposable one-time use, a kleenex represents everything that Lorde thinks militates against the erotic: consumerism, conformism, impersonalism. Rather than a disposable kleenex, the erotic is a communal tapestry.

So, too, is what Madonna aims for in *Erotica*: not sensation but feeling, and not individual but communal. Once more, to return to "Deeper and Deeper" and the opening lines that repeat throughout: *Deeper and deeper and deeper and deeper*. It's not just that these lines about *deeper and deeper* speak the language of Lorde's erotic. They also, notably, do not have any personal pronouns or people attached. It's not "*I feel* it deeper and deeper" or "*She's* never gonna hide it again." This is pure feeling, something felt and shared across bodies.

So, too, in the most elegiac song, the one devoted to her friends lost to AIDS, "In This Life." Here, we do have pronouns but still an invitation into community: *Have you ever watched your best friend die? Have you ever watched a grown man cry? . . . Why do we have to pretend?* By beginning with two questions, Madonna is treating her song like an

[19]Ibid., 58.

invitation to group therapy, a support group. This is a song that creates a "we" who will not "have to pretend" any more. For another feeling that can be felt "deeper and deeper" is one of grief. And when it is felt deeply, when it is felt truly and with others on the dance floor, grief, too, is erotic.

2
Subculture/Pop Culture

Before *Erotica*, there was *Sex*. In the previous chapter, I explored how the music album departs from the coffee table book—as well as the movie that completed Madonna's 1992–3 season of engineered sexual controversy, *Body of Evidence*—because of its more sentimental relation to sex or at least a desire for safe sex in the context of chronic mourning as governmental neglect and social stigma allowed HIV/AIDS to decimate queer and marginalized communities. Because *Sex* was so sensational, it shaded how people listened to *Erotica*, which made it hard for them to notice the difference in politics and in content between the two. Madonna told *TIME Magazine* about the timing: "Most people want to hear me say I regret putting out my *Sex* book. I don't. What was problematic was putting out my *Erotica* album at the same time. I loved that record, and it was overlooked. Everything I did for the next three years was dwarfed by my book."[1] By regretting the timing of the book, Madonna suggests the

[1]Quoted in Taraborrelli, *Madonna: An Intimate Biography of an Icon at Sixty*, 237.

extent to which, to her but unlike to the fan base to which she promoted them, the book and the album were not a package deal. They aimed to accomplish different things in different ways. If in the previous chapter, that difference was about Madonna's relation to sex, in this chapter it is about her relation to subcultures and especially the queer of color communities and underground spaces of cultural production from which she drew, or sometimes appropriated, inspiration.

In their short book review of *Sex* in the December 10, 1992, issue, *Rolling Stone* had this to say of the images: "the campy fashion-ad photos, by Robert Mapplethorpe-wanna-be Steven Meisel, reveal Madonna's fondness for Vanilla Ice, lesbian skinheads, Latin males, black rubber, group gropes, golden retrievers and pizza."[2] It's the jibe at photographer Meisel that stings more than the flippant list of Madonna's desires. Meisel has had a successful fashion-ad photography career, to the point that Franca Sozzani, the editor-in-chief of Italian *Vogue*, tapped him for almost every issue cover until she died in 2016, and it is a career that has been at many stages boosted by Madonna, beginning with his shoot of the cover for the *Like a Virgin* album. He knows fashion. But it is the "ad" that fashion attaches to in "fashion-ad" that suggests its distance from something like art. This is photography that is commercial, rather than elevated—that is sold by the street magazine vendor rather than Christie's or Sotheby's. He is, this reviewer suggests, art-aspirational, a "Mapplethorpe-wanna-be."

---

[2]"Books," *Rolling Stone*, no. 645/646 (December 10, 1992).

In 1992, lots of folks wanted to be Mapplethorpe, the photographer whose work, in an exhibit that toured the year of his death from AIDS in 1989, was at the center of a national conversation about sex, art, and the public sphere. In the 1970s and 1980s, Mapplethorpe had built a career out of black-and-white erotic portraits of the New York queer landscape, including people tied up in S&M scenes or individual bodies arranged like statuary, their buttocks chiseled in classical proportions. At one point he was the official photographer of Mineshaft, a members-only gay leather bar in Manhattan. A retrospective of his career curated by Janet Kardon of Philadelphia's Institute of Contemporary Art began touring in the summer of 1989, with a stop planned at D.C.'s Corcoran Gallery of Art, to be supported by a grant from the National Endowment for the Arts (NEA)—which meant tax dollars were involved. Under pressure from religious groups and conservative organizations, the show at Corcoran was ultimately canceled, Mapplethorpe's works labeled obscenity rather than art, and therefore something in which the "public" government had no legitimate reason to invest its tax revenue.

During the Reagan administration of the 1980s, art had become a proxy battle for larger questions of who gets to be a part of a "public": public assistance (the racist demonization of the "welfare queen"), public education (whose religions are protected over the debates involving school prayer), and public opinion (whose ideologies warrant political representation and whose are obscene and should be censored). Perhaps most public of these battles concerned the sculptor Richard Serra's *Tilted Arc*, 120 feet of curved, 12-foot tall steel embedded in 1981 in the concrete of the Jacob K. Javitis Federal Building plaza in Manhattan, commissioned by the United States General Services Administration (GSA) on recommendation by the NEA. The sculpture, as imagined by Serra, was not just the steel but the entire range of movements it enabled and impeded in the plaza: the work of art was not just the object but how people moved and reacted to it. But soon after its installation, it came under attack precisely because it impeded easy access to the building. Stationed in the building adjacent, the chief judge of the US Court of International Trade, Edward D. Re, found it sufficiently disruptive of his daily routine to demand its removal. In 1985, the GSA appointed a panel of five to decide the fate of the sculpture, which it viewed as its private property according to the contract they had signed with Serra. Even though more than two-thirds of the 180 people who testified at the hearing were in favor of keeping the sculpture, the panel voted to destroy it. Indeed, the public panel, like so many of the arguments against the sculpture, was more a farce of publicness than a forum for it. In any case, the show trial having affirmed a government decision reached ahead of the public process, and Serra having lost all subsequent appeals, *Tilted Arc* was removed from the plaza in 1989. Arguing against the property terms in which the debate had been cast—whether or not the government had a right to destroy property it had purchased for the public—Serra simply remarked that the "government by destroying *Tilted Arc* violated my right to free speech."[3]

[3]Richard Serra, "Art and Censorship," *Critical Inquiry* 17, no. 3 (1991): 578.

Free speech is not just an individual right but a collective right. Serra's larger complaint in the *Tilted Arc* controversy was over the exclusionary moves that constructed a public as a universal, consensual singularity, a move that, in censoring the work of gay artists like Robert Mapplethorpe, was also saying gays were not part of the public sphere; in the government negligence of the AIDS epidemic, it was not too far-fetched to say the government was actively deleting gays from the public sphere. Instead of viewing the public as a sphere that is fragmented and characterized by difference and disagreement, the government tried to remove sources of dissent in order to maintain its fantasy of consensus.

To be a "Mapplethorpe wanna-be" in 1990 was to aspire not only to Mapplethorpe's status as an artist but to his position in a larger debate over obscenity. It was to want not only to make good art but to be at the center of a national conversation. It was to aspire to being something Congress would spend committee sessions looking at and talking about. Something that is censored is, of course, something everyone is talking about. This aspiration in *Sex* is evidenced not only in its black-and-white photographs of erotic scenes in the style of Mapplethorpe but also in its religious imagery. The other "public" controversy the year of Mapplethorpe's dealt with Andres Serrano's *Piss Christ*, which photographed a miniature crucifix submerged in the artist's urine, glowing amber orange in the photo. This is the sacred meeting the profane, but the large glossy Cibachrome print also makes the profane sacred again, this time not in the register of religion but in the register of a Hollywood movie poster or a magazine advertisement produced on Madison Avenue—

capitalism is the new religion and advertisement its new magical spectacle.

In *Sex*, the singer of "Like a Prayer" and "Papa Don't Preach" is also shot beneath a crucifix, while on the floor a lover assumes the crucified pose flanked by votive candles (that also, when quickly skimming through, almost look like bottles of poppers). But the commentary that comes from meeting the sacred and the profane and the question of who counts in the public sphere are blurred in the hands of a *Vogue* photographer whose job has always been to sell magazines, rather than secure a grant from the NEA. Here is an aspiration for controversy as a recoding of the commercial impulse, an alibi for market forces, and a substitute for aesthetic achievement.

Yet there is one more thing that *Sex* also retains from the Mapplethorpe approach to subject matter, perhaps most evident in a series of pages toward the end where Madonna seems to live out an island fantasy with a man and woman of color: first, white meat in a sandwich, then, standing over the woman who lies down, spraying suntan lotion from a bottle like Madonna's ejaculating on her. Hilton Als, the *New Yorker* cultural critic, has said of viewing Mapplethorpe's photographs of Black men arranged as statues: "I saw myself reduced to Black and gay. Not a self, just Black and gay."[4] A reduction to a sexual subject is part of what is going on in *Sex*, too, although Madonna might say she is reducing herself in addition to Black models. What is also going on, though, is

[4]Quoted in Carter Ratcliff, "Robert Mapplethorpe: Obsession and Mastery," *The Brooklyn Rail* (December 2019).

the invocation of miscegenation as an underlying controversy that has been sublimated into S&M to find a voice for itself. In 1992, interracial relations—and marriage, long after the Supreme Court decision decriminalizing it in *Loving v. Virginia* in 1967—are officially not taboo; lots of people, almost everyone in certain political constituencies, are still against it, but what's taboo now is *saying* you are, just as many sitting senators supported segregation but would not admit it now. The worst thing you can be is racist. But when there is an official taboo, when there is an official population or sexual practice you're allowed to hate—queer communities, S&M sex—it becomes a site for that repressed battle to play out.

On Mapplethorpe, Judith Butler said in 1990 that the "naked Black men characterized by Mapplethorpe engage a certain racist romanticism of Black men's excessive physicality and sexual readiness, their photographic currency as a sexual sign."[5] This is part of "perhaps the most offensive dimension of Mapplethorpe's work," which is not the queer obscenity named by senators like the North Carolinian Jesse Helms, who led the charge against NEA grantees: "the fear of miscegenation operates tacitly here as well, disavowed, contained, and deferred by the stated spectre of 'homoeroticism.'"[6] As I explore throughout this chapter and continue into the next, Madonna's music had its desired controversial impact in the 1990s because of its own

---

[5]Judith Butler, "The Force of Fantasy: Feminism, Mapplethorpe, and Discursive Excess," *differences: A Journal of Feminist Cultural Studies* 2, no. 2 (July 1, 1990): 118.

[6]Ibid., 119.

way of mixing and remixing the sexual and the racial, all in the service of the "art" to which she aspired. This means her appropriative relationship is not just about race but about politics and business. Or rather, this white woman's relation to Black and queer cultural materials is also the relation of a mainstream pop culture industry to politics—to the specter of racial and sexual revolution and freedom.

* * *

In 1990, the white lesbian filmmaker Jennie Livingston premiered what would become the most influential LGBTQ documentary, *Paris Is Burning*, which explores the New York City drag ball culture that created the "vogue" dance that, also in 1990, inspired Madonna's song of the same name, a house dance track that would go on to be one of her most popular. The balls, organized by the Black and Latinx gay and transgender communities in Harlem, staged competitions for participants to "walk" in a particular "category," performing through dress and action the look and mannerisms of, for instance, "town and country," "executive realness," or "schoolboy/school girl realness." Marked by race and class, these are lifestyle and identity categories from which the primarily poor and queer ball attendees are excluded in US culture. Many kicked out of the homes of their biological families because of their queer identities, the individuals who walk in the categories also represented "houses" established and led by drag "mothers," creating an alternative form of kinship that provides support, care, and belonging amid larger structures of racial and sexual inequality.

Paris Is Burning has been a central topic of discussion in queer studies not only because of its survey of a resilient queer underground and kinship network but also because of the complicated dynamic between the film's director and the film's subjects. Livingston, who may share a larger coalitional identity with the house members—an umbrella now expressed in the acronym LGBTQ—was nonetheless not from their immediate community, and as a white woman who had just graduated from Yale, she had easier access to the very categories her film subjects performed from a position of structural distance. Livingston never appears on screen in the film, giving the impression of being an anthropologist who has parachuted in to document some exotic other. In an essay that asked "Is Paris Burning?," the Black feminist theorist and writer bell hooks noted that Livingston's visual absence from the film screen makes it "easy for viewers to imagine that they are watching an ethnographic film documenting the life of black gay 'natives' and not recognize that they are watching a work shaped and formed by a perspective and standpoint specific to Livingston."[7] In particular, this specifically white standpoint could not see that the femininity toward which many of the ball performers aspired was itself a specifically white femininity—the one that would adorn the covers of a magazine like *Vogue* in the first place.

[7] bell hooks, *Black Looks: Race and Representation* (Boston, MA: South End Press, 1992), 151.

Had Livingston approached her subject with greater awareness of the way white supremacy shapes cultural production—determining not only what representations of blackness are deemed acceptable, marketable, as well worthy of seeing—perhaps the film would not so easily have turned the black drag ball into a spectacle for the entertainment of those presumed to be on the outside of this experience looking in.[8]

In 1993, Judith Butler published a partial defense of *Paris Is Burning* in their monograph *Bodies That Matter*, a follow-up to the 1990 volume *Gender Trouble*, which is often considered an opening to the new academic field that would come to be called "queer theory." In that earlier volume, Butler had argued that gender is "performative," which is distinct from a conscious "performance" that an actor does on stage. A performative speech act is something that creates the reality it names. For instance, the city clerk's "I now pronounce you man and wife" creates the marriage it talks about. Butler said gender is similarly performative because it is created by the continual utterance of norms, from the clothes people wear to the social roles they take up:

> Gender is performative insofar as it is the effect of a regulatory regime of gender differences in which genders are divided and hierarchized under constraint. Social constraints, taboos, prohibitions, threats of punishment operate in the ritualized repetition of norms, and this

[8]Ibid., 152.

repetition constitutes the temporalized scene of gender construction and destabilization. There is no subject who precedes or enacts this repetition of norms.[9]

To say gender is performative means that gender does not exist before these actions; it is not like someone has a gender and then consciously chooses to express it, but rather that their actions are constantly creating the gender they are ascribed. One agenda for queer analysis would be to explore how we are always constrained by the norms that came before us, which shape our performance of gender. Another agenda is to explore how new kinds of gender are opened up by surprising or ironic performances.

This is where drag comes in. One way of recasting the Black queer performance of white femininity is to say it is less about cementing the supremacy of whiteness and more about showing how illegitimate that whiteness is, how its power is founded on repeated performance. When someone who is not white performs whiteness, whiteness itself is brought into crisis, and so the drag balls, Butler would say, denaturalize the categories they simultaneously perform: "*Paris Is Burning* might be understood as repetitions of hegemonic forms of power which fail to repeat loyally and, in that failure, open possibilities for resignifying the terms of violation against their violating aims."[10] And yet,

---

[9]Judith Butler, "Critically Queer," *GLQ: A Journal of Lesbian and Gay Studies* 1, no. 1 (1993): 21.

[10]Judith Butler, *Bodies That Matter: On the Discursive Limits of "Sex"* (New York: Routledge, 2011), 84.

Butler acknowledges, the increased threat of mortality these marginalized communities encounter—whether premature death from hate crimes against trans people or premature death from incomplete access to health care, particularly in the context of HIV/AIDS—"calls into question whether parodying the dominant norms is enough to displace them."[11]

What Butler is ultimately interested in is what they call "appropriation," a word they use in at least two ways in their chapter on *Paris Is Burning*. One is a kind of symbolic appropriation of the "norm," when someone replicates or performs a normative subject position, like in queer communities that appropriate the language of the "family" to describe a non-biological kinship. Another is a kind of economic appropriation when one social group takes and profits from materials from another social group, like when a white filmmaker makes a movie about people of color and earns money and awards from it. Both of these forms of appropriation are related to but different from the "cultural appropriation" that we more commonly talk about in everyday life these days, like when a white person wears a sombrero "for Halloween." One task for analyzing the work of someone like Livingston—and also Madonna, who, like Livingston, may share overlapping identities with queer dance communities but remains in a position of privilege to dip in and out—is to track the interactions between symbolic, economic, and cultural appropriation.

[11]Ibid., 85.

In an academic article published the summer before *Erotica* came out, the art history and Renaissance studies professor Carla Freccerro noted possible connections between the Italian heritage of Madonna the singer and Black Madonnas, paintings or figurines in which the Virgin Mary is depicted as Black. During the Renaissance, "Italian immigrants were often associated with Africans by their northern compatriots, by the Protestant majority, and by the established Catholic church. Chromatically black Madonnas and saints abound in southern Italian and Catholic worship."[12] In the twentieth century, Freccerro notes that "Italian Harlem shared borders with Black Harlem in New York," where Madonna first moved looking for a big break after a brief stint at the University of Michigan:

> as in many urban communities across the United States, Italians and African Americans share a long American history of similarities and differences, conflicts and cooperations. For Madonna, there is, additionally, a personal narrative of guilt assuaged, in that Steven Bray, an African American R&B musician, composer, songwriter, and producer, gave her her first break into the business. . . . She subsequently abandoned him for a producer with more prestige.[13]

Before her face adorned the cover of her eponymous first album, it was absent from the cover of the first single

[12]Carla Freccero, "Our Lady of MTV: Madonna's 'Like a Prayer,'" *boundary 2* 19, no. 2 (1992): 179.

[13]Ibid., 173.

released from that album, "Everybody," not because she was too hideous to appear but because the record producers, according to her unofficial biographers, "didn't want people to know she was white."[14] Madonna herself has said, in a 1989 *Rolling Stone* profile when asked if she ever "feels black":

When I was a little girl, I wished I was black. All my girlfriends were black. I was living in Pontiac, Michigan, and I was definitely the minority in the neighborhood. White people were scarce there. All of my friends were black, and all the music I listened to was black. I was incredibly jealous of all my black girlfriends because they could have braids in their hair that stuck up everywhere. So I would go through this incredible ordeal of putting wire in my hair and braiding it so that I could make *my* hair stick up. I used to make cornrows and everything. But if being black is synonymous with having soul, then, yes, I feel that I am.[15]

In *The Girlie Show*, the tour that brought *Erotica*'s songs to the stage, a different hair fetishism is achieved: she opens the second act by descending on a disco ball with a massive white afro.

In her approach to race as braided hair and "having soul," Madonna speaks the language of cultural appropriation while not quite noting that what separates her from her Black girlfriends is not just cornrows but economic

---

[14]Taraborrelli, *Madonna: An Intimate Biography of an Icon at Sixty*.

[15]Bill Zehme, "Madonna: The *Rolling Stone* Interview," *Rolling Stone*, no. 548 (March 23, 1989).

opportunity and mobility. For the purpose of something like *Sex*, what also seems important to note is a different accessibility of performing sexuality itself, with Black women historically stereotyped and hypersexualized by a larger white culture. For Madonna, a young white woman, promiscuity, multiple sexual partners, and non-normative sex look liberating, something about owning her body and femininity. But coming right after the presidential administration of Ronald Reagan, who had popularized the term "welfare queen" as one way of blaming Black poverty on single Black mothers, this same performance of sexuality can be pathologizing.

Often mediating between the white woman and the Black girlfriend in these questions of appropriation is the position of the Asian woman, who unlike the "normal" white woman or the "hypersexualized" Black woman is often cast in mainstream US culture as undersexual, asexual: repressed rather than oversexual, too submissive rather than too aggressive. An article in the September 10, 1989, issue of *Rolling Stone* followed Madonna while touring in Japan, calling her the "icon of Western fixations." After she has to cancel a show in the Korakuen stadium in Tokyo because of a typhoon, sparking riots, Madonna is encountered by a local young female fan, and the journalist with her takes great pains to describe the "Japanese girl's" performance of deference: "she clasps Madonna's hands and kneels before her, bowing her head, tears falling from her eyes." She "seems to be embarrassed at how she is presenting herself." When asked why she thinks she is so popular in Japan, Madonna reflects:

I think I stand for a lot of things in their minds. . . . You know, a lot of kinds of stereotypes, like the whole sex-goddess image and the blond thing. But mainly I think they feel that most of my music is really, really positive, and I think they appreciate that, particularly the women. I think I stand for everything that they're really taught to *not* be, so maybe I provide them with a little bit of encouragement.[16]

In Madonna's thought process, if Black women are oversexualized, Asian women are undersexualized and in need of more sexual liberation. She is the one to liberate them.

On *Erotica*, this comes out especially in the music video for "Rain." As I examined in the previous chapter, this is the song that closes down the sexiness in the opening act of *Erotica* on stage in *The Girlie Show*. It's unique on the album for its New Age influences, its ambient noise. *Billboard* has said of the song that a "slow and seductive rhyme base surrounded by cascading, sparkling synths inspires a sweet and charming vocal."[17] For the music video, Madonna tapped Mark Romanek, mostly known in the 1990s for music videos, before he would go on to direct such features as *Never Let Me Go*, based on Japanese-born author Kazuo Ishiguro's quasi-science fiction novel about human cloning. In the "Rain"

[16]Mikal Gilmore, "The Madonna Mystique," *Rolling Stone*, no. 508 (September 10, 1987).

[17]Larry Flick, "Single Reviews—Pop: Madonna, Rain," *Billboard* (July 10, 1993).

video, Madonna is on a film shoot—dancing in artificial rain before there is the rise of artificial sun—being directed by a character played by the Japanese composer Ryuichi Sakamoto, a champion and developer of new electronic music genres but probably best known in the United States in 1992 for having recently written the score for *The Last Emperor* along with David Byrne and Cong Su. The film's crew depicted in the music video is primarily Japanese (kanji are printed on the clapperboard along with "Madonna" and "Rain"), often seen either crouching around Sakamoto's character or on computers adjusting sound and light.

Romanek later explained, "I came up with the basic idea of setting it in Tokyo and showing the film crew. It was very Zen, very stripped away. She was this accessible, vulnerable creature surrounded by the high-tech and the global."[18] The explanation is telling for what it confirms about the US perception of Japan in the 1990s. Japan stands in for what might seem an unlikely combination of minimalism usually coded as spiritual in some way ("very Zen") and the hyper-vanguard of technology. Ironically, the cultural marking of "very Zen" is also what "the high-tech and the global" sometimes seeks to erase, giving the sense of a culture-less cosmopolitan taste. Sleek black-and-white lines, polished surfaces, clean lighting: these fill luxury hotels from Paris to Tokyo so that someone traveling with a multinational corporation can feel relatively at home in each location, like not too much has changed from one business day to another.

---

[18]Maureen Sajbel, "Video Vogue: A Vulnerable Madonna," *Los Angeles Times* (July 28, 1993).

Japan stands in as the source for this kind of future style as omni-style.[19]

In the video-within-a-video, Madonna is primarily singing alone, but there is a male love interest with whom she blurrily makes out. Intercut with these images are those of Japanese staff women working on computers, moving around charts and graphs and numbers, close-ups of hands typing on keyboards. It is not clear what these charts are doing for video production, but this also seems typical of early 1990s representations of computers, when there isn't always a match between what's on the screen and the function the computer is supposed to be serving. In any case, what is striking is the association not just of Japan but of the Japanese with technology, the blending together of Japanese hands and Japanese machines. It also implies a difference in eroticization: Madonna, with her love interest and her dancing, stands in for the body, whereas these Japanese women stand in for the mind, somehow de-eroticized in the service of Madonna's eroticization.

"Rain" is also notable for a middle sequence in which the synths seem to turbo-charge. In the music video, this sequence arrives as the lights are turned up on stage, leaving Madonna basking in artificial sun (as she sings, *here comes the sun . . .*) and the director and staff, behind the lights, looking on through sunglasses, as if to avoid being blinded.

---

[19]On the prehistory of the West's fascination with Japan as offering an unexpectedly universal aesthetic, "*modern*, but *not in the way everybody else is*," see Grace Elisabeth Lavery, *Quaint, Exquisite: Victorian Aesthetics and the Idea of Japan* (Princeton, NJ: Princeton University Press, 2019), 28.

There is also a costume change. In the first half, Madonna wears minimalist black garb provided by Japanese designer Rei Kawakubo of Comme des Garcons; now she wears white provided by Vivienne Westwood, perhaps best known for her earlier association with English punk. It is a probably unintentional, but still uncomfortable, allegory, the movement from black to white, rain to sun, also literally represented by a movement from Asian to European textiles.

In the imagination of "Rain," the music video, Japanese technology and people work hard to make Madonna look good, but they must themselves remain off screen, not main characters in a love story. They must remain somehow servile like the "Japanese girl" who ran into Madonna after the canceled concert in the *Rolling Stone* profile. The music video captures something specific about the 1992 moment in globalization: the role Japan plays in a global imagination of being both ahead of the times in technology and somehow, in order to be so, post-culture, unseen, unmarked.

* * *

Another visual reference that the iconography of Madonna's "Vogue" music video and *The Girlie Show* tour make, through the triangulation *Erotica* provides, is to the emerging "New Queer Cinema," a term coined by the film studies scholar B. Ruby Rich in an issue of *Sight and Sound* just two months before *Erotica* itself was released. She was referring to a number of underground or indie films that had begun to tell queer stories in the later 1980s and early 1990s. One of the most influential of these films was Isaac Julien's impressionistic, black-and-white 1989 film, *Looking for Langston*. The title refers to Langston Hughes, the Harlem Renaissance poet often held out in gay circles as a gay father figure: a successful and influential Black man who likely had sex with men in the first half of the twentieth century, before the advent of the modern gay rights movement in the second half of the century. In 1989, Julien is looking for Hughes because he is also looking for a Black queer history, a past to connect to the present.

The atmospheric film clearly influenced David Fincher's video for "Vogue": its black-and-white lushness, the clothing and settings of the primarily Black dancers. Julien's film ends with a police mob crashing a nightclub—a ballroom from an era before the ballrooms of *Paris Is Burning*. The dance floor has been evacuated before they get in, and Julien refuses to depict the violence of gay-bashing. But right before the evacuation, the dancers, twirling in communal ecstasy, throw shot glasses to the ground. It's an oblique reference to Marsha P. Johnson's "shotglass heard around the world." According to legend (Johnson actually denies the account), on June 29, 1969, as police stormed the Stonewall Inn that had become a congregating spot for queer people in New York City, the Black, gender non-conforming, self-identifying "drag queen" threw a shotglass at a mirror and joined other patrons in taking a stand, fighting back against the queerphobic police brutality. Although certainly not the first in LGBTQ history, the riots that ensued are taken as a symbolic origin moment for the modern queer movement.

Julien enforced the linking of dance, politics, and history with a voice-over accompanying this scene precipitating a riot, borrowed from the Black gay poet Essex Hemphill:

> Men whose lusty hearts weakened
> in the middle of the night,
> and brought them to tears,
> to their knees
> for their former lovers.
> They could look at me and tell
> they did not want to endure
> what beauty love scars give me.
> So touch me now —
> Hannibal, Toussaint.
> I am a revolution without bloodshed.[20]

Hannibal and Toussaint are historical military leaders: the former noted for leading Carthage in a battle against the Roman Republic and the latter for being a leader of the Haitian Revolution. Both are, in other words, noted for anti-imperialist campaigns. Hemphill's speaker, a Black gay man in the present, identifies in this tradition, linking antiracist and pro-queer political agendas in a new "revolution" that is firmly rooted in a sexual liberation.

Like Julien, Madonna likes to overlap historical periods—from Harlem Renaissance to 1960s Stonewall and back to ancient Rome—a tendency I'll explore further in the next chapter. However, as Cindy Patton puts it in her discussion

---

[20]Essex Hemphill, *Conditions: Poems* (Washington, D.C.: Be Bop Books, 1986), 14.

of the "Vogue" music video as part of the academic collection of essays on Madonna published the same year as *Erotica*, Madonna mostly devises a "simulation of history": the music video "creates a memory link—a simultaneity—to specific historical times without constructing a place of memory."[21] In contrast, in the hands of a Black queer person like Julien or Hemphill, this promiscuity with history is also a project of inventing the history from which they have been canonically excluded: their stories less often recorded in the annals of history, they are writing this history, speculating this history, for the very first time in the present. Not preserved in the official institutions of the library or archive, or even in the oral histories preserved by heterosexuality—the stories parents tell their children—this Black queer history is instead precariously preserved through something more like word of mouth. As the queer theorists Lauren Berlant and Michael Warner would put it in a famous article a few years later: "Contexts of queer world making depend on parasitic and fugitive elaboration through gossip, dance clubs, softball leagues, and the phone-sex ads that increasingly are the commercial support for print-mediated left culture in general."[22]

Julien is acutely sensitive to the tension between underground social space—like the queer ballroom—and mainstream "commercial support." He is also acutely aware of how mis-

[21]Cindy Patton, "Embodying Subaltern Memory," in *The Madonna Connection: Representational Politics, Subcultural Identities, and Cultural Theory*, ed. Cathy Schwichtenberg (Boulder, CO: Westview Press, 1993), 98.

[22]Lauren Berlant and Michael Warner, "Sex in Public," *Critical Inquiry* 24, no. 2 (1998): 561.

calibrating the balance between the underground and the commercial can be a threat to the underground. This is not just in the case of selling out, the commercialization of previously subversive cultural practices. It is also in the case alluded to by the mob at the end of *Looking for Langston*: more publicity of an underground space also advertises it for violent backlash. More visibility is not always liberating. Sometimes, it comes with a bull's-eye. The difficult strategic question is how to redirect commercial impulses into the maintenance of precarious spaces and cultures, without heightening that precarity through newly public means of exploitation and oppression.

It is on this question of strategy that Jeanne Livingston in *Paris Is Burning* and Madonna in her various works inspired by vogueing, including *Erotica*'s sampling of "Vogue" and *The Girlie Show*'s use of its aesthetics on stage, show a certain insensitivity. Put another way, Madonna desires the revolutionary spirit of the ballroom, desires to allude to the slave revolt of a Toussaint, but underestimates the challenging nature of fighting a revolution, of making strategic compromises, of balancing fugitivity and holding ground, of nourishing the privacy and exclusivity of a safe space, and of publicizing the intervention that space makes in the larger mainstream world. She wants the atmosphere of liberation, but nowhere is there the related sense of liberation's violent backlash: all representation is good representation.

* * *

Erotica evidences Madonna's attraction to, but strategic distance from, queer communities and communities of color in its sound, particularly its samples, sometimes unauthorized, of other singers and song traditions. The album is full of sonic appropriations, in the three senses explored earlier: symbolic, economic, cultural. In the remainder of this chapter, let me move us through a listening tour of these sampled sounds. Cumulatively, Madonna's appropriations reveal a threefold theory of the erotic:

1. The erotic is exotic.
2. The erotic is nostalgic.
3. The erotic needs an exotic, nostalgic soundtrack to get you in the mood.

1. The Erotic Is Exotic.

As Madonna first sings *Erotica, romance . . .* on the album's title track, a riff that repeats throughout the song samples Kool & the Gang's "Jungle Boogie," the popular funk track from 1973. The song is one of the most memorable from the New Jersey-founded band, played throughout nightclubs the decade it hit the radios. It's a bit too old for it to have been a soundtrack in the clubs Madonna frequented, but by having the sample in the background throughout the song, she acknowledges the dance floor is where, to play off another song in the album, *my love is, where love begins.* This is also a specifically funky dance floor, one whose sounds come from a jazz and R&B tradition rather than more immediately from contemporary pop. At the same time that this suggests Madonna's indebtedness to Black musicians, it suggests how much the erotic is, for Madonna, always a bit in the past, not at the cutting edge of dance music but in the sultry hangover from last night's hits.

"Jungle Boogie" is also a lesson in eclecticism, a stylistic teacher for Madonna. Lyrically, the song was originally not just sung by the band's roadie Don Boyce but spoken, scatted, and groaned. Throughout *Erotica*, Madonna also breaks into spoken sequences, half-hearted raps, and, of course, orgasmic moans. The "Jungle" of the title is memorably delivered in a Tarzan yell near the track's conclusion, cementing a longing gaze toward somewhere vaguely in Africa. This, too, is a move Madonna borrows and adapts in her own way in the song's coda. If "Jungle Boogie" has its Tarzan yell toward the end, "Erotica" has an Easter chant ("El Yom 'Ulliqa 'Ala Khashaba") from the Lebanese singer Nouhad Wadie' Haddad, known as Fairuz. One of the most popular singers of the Arab world, Fairuz has been called the "soul of Lebanon," which is perhaps why, after Fairuz sued Madonna in 1993 for the unauthorized sample—they settled out of court for $2.5 million—Lebanon was not shy to ban Madonna's album for sale in the country. The Arabic portion Madonna samples, while she repeats *all over me* from the line *Put your hands all over me*, translates to "Today, he is held to the cross." Throughout her career, Madonna has often put herself on a cross in performances, and in the context of the culture wars of the 1980s and 1990s, we know, as I mentioned earlier in this chapter, that Andres Serrano had already done the definitive move in 1987 when he submerged one in a bottle of his own piss and called it, creatively, *Piss Christ*. But it is probably the sound, rather than the lyrics, that mattered to Madonna in her sample of Fairuz's rendition of the events of Good Friday. Assuming an audience who would not themselves know Arabic, or the chant tradition from which this particular sample derives, the singing offers something, like Kool & the Gang's Tarzan yell, vaguely exotic and therefore something that keeps the feeling of the erotic going.

The flamenco instrumental break in "Deeper and Deeper" is also a continuation of the erotic. This surprise break comes after the song's bridge, which talks of a love that can't be explained but which she refuses to hide. Enter the flamenco: a way of showing off a feeling without words, just rhythm. Madonna's producer Shep Pettibone originally resisted adding the guitar and the castanets: "I didn't like the idea of taking a Philly house song and putting 'La Isla Bonita' in the middle of it, but that's what she wanted so that's what she got!"[23] We've moved from the jungles of Africa to Spain's Andalusia, and Latin allusion stands in for the *romance* that *someone said was dead*. The music video for "La Isla Bonita" from five years prior gives insight into Madonna's imagination of people and romance. She plays two characters: one a devout Catholic in all white, in a drab room; the other a flamenco dancer, red dress matching the red flames of the brightly lit room in which she dances. For Madonna, this is what flamenco, by way of its stereotypical Latin passion, means: sexual liberation.

So, too, with the reggae sounds on "Why's It So Hard." This song doesn't have a direct sample from another song, but it does begin with and carry throughout reggae allusions,

[23]Quoted in Marc Andrews, *Madonna: Song by Song* (Stroud, England: Fonthill Media, 2022), 61.

much like the flamenco brought in for "Deeper and Deeper." Madonna explained about the composition of the song: "Shep happened to go to Jamaica and I happened to go scuba diving in the Cayman Islands, and both places are heavily reggae-based cultures. That's what we came back having listened to, so we decided out of nowhere to do a reggae track."[24] Madonna's appropriations often look like this: a sound she picked up from somewhere, although more often that somewhere is a dance floor, whether the discos of the 1970s or the emerging electronic scene of the 1990s. By 1992, reggae already had an established Western presence; in 1985, the Grammy Awards had introduced the Award for Best Reggae Album, particularly after reggae had made influences on punk rock in the UK. But the genre's indelible associations with the African diaspora and pan-Africanism make its influence on this particular Madonna song, about cross-racial love and solidarity, seem both appropriate and misjudged. It is appropriate for a white listener who associates anything Black with a politics of integration and inclusion, which is what makes possible appropriation in the first place, misjudged as tribute rather than theft.

The use of the culturally specific "other" to stand in for a kind of universal "everyone love one another" ethic is a common move in appropriation. What is missing from the move is a kind of reciprocity: the dominant culture's inclusion of subcultural materials is its way of holding up the dominant culture as representation of all, even if it remains controlled

---

[24]Ibid., 65.

by the dominant class, even as it does not reciprocate with materials for a subculture to exploit and profit off of. Put another way: a multinational organization can keep itself profitable by finding more and more materials to use, more and more places to set up shop, and more and more people to sell things to. This is why McDonalds can start selling a Teriyaki McBurger in Tokyo. But this is different, in fact the opposite, from a multinational organization redistributing wealth to places outside its country of headquarters, like subsidizing Japanese farmers who harvest what goes into the McBurger. Madonna, the tourist, goes to the Caribbean and brings back reggae to put on her menu.

2. The Erotic Is Nostalgic.

Madonna also appropriates from herself or songs previously written for her. The title of "Waiting" alludes to the chorus of her earlier erotic track "Justify My Love": *Wanting, needing, waiting for you to justify my love.* Madonna makes something auto-erotic in the self-allusion, something that feels like all she had been waiting for all along was herself. "Justify My Love" was the most important new single on Madonna's 1990 *Immaculate Collection* album, which began with remixes of fifteen of her greatest hits to date. With "Justify My Love," Madonna worked with Lenny Kravitz and met the musician with whom he was having an affair, Ingrid Chavez, who would go on to produce some of the tracks on *Erotica*. For the backbone of "Justify My Love," Kravitz sampled from Public Enemy's "Security of the First World," and the band's lawyers were not amused. For his part, Kravitz's lawyer

Stephen Smith thought Public Enemy had in turn sampled from James Brown's 1969 "Funky Drummer," arguing that "If there is a lawsuit, it should be by James Brown."

There's a more important lawsuit and dynamic of appropriation, though: Chavez was originally uncredited as a writer of "Justify My Love" and eventually won a large settlement for the oversight. In her 1991 eponymous debut album, Chavez had originally intended to set her spoken word poetry to music from Prince, and this is the most important thing Madonna seems to learn from the eventually messy "Justify My Love" collaboration: the use of spoken voice to make things sexy. "Justify" begins with a monologue of spoken desires: *I want to kiss you in Paris. I want to hold your hand in Rome. I want to run naked in a rainstorm. Make love in a train cross-country.* Madonna is at her most forthright when she's speaking, rather than singing. Not so much in *Erotica*, though. "Waiting," too, begins with a spoken verse: *Well, I know from experience that if you have to ask for something more than once or twice, it wasn't yours in the first place. And that's hard to accept when you love someone and you're led to believe in their moment of need that they want what you want but they don't.* This verse is definitely less horny—too needy, too unspecific on when and where the lover is going to be kissed.

The sultry, opening horns and drums for "Waiting" are both also borrowed, the horns from "Sneakin' in the Back" by a band headed by Tom Scott, a member of the Blues Brothers; and the drums from "Papa Was Too" by Joe Tex, who was known for his Southern soul. The horns are most memorable, and the phrase "Sneakin' in the Back" would of course have had a memorable double meaning for a gay listener (not to mention "Papa Was Too"). But "Sneakin' in the Back" is purely instrumental, and Madonna's adoption for "Waiting" suggests that her longing for her inattentive lover is also a bit like being kept a secret, an affair hidden away, a lover sneaking on the side, instead of out in the open. Most importantly, it keeps us waiting again back in the mid-1970s, the historical center of gravity for this album's sampled sounds. Waiting, for Madonna, is also a nostalgia, not a looking forward to something hoped-for but a looking backward at something lost, something haunting the air from a previous time.

Another look back comes in "Bye Bye Baby," the third track on *Erotica*, with its background sample of "Woo! Yeah!" shouts that made Lyn Collins's song "Think (About It)" popular after it was produced by James Brown in 1972. Madonna sustains the funk of that period with which she began the album. Madonna is also hardly the first to sample the song, suggesting less a direct citation of or indebtedness to Collins and more an invocation of the dance floors of the 1980s and 1990s in which her sample already circulated prolifically and decontextualized. In 1986, "Think (About It)" appeared on the popular compilation series *Ultimate Breaks and Beats*, which became a treasure trove of songs to sample for hip-hop producers throughout the remainder of the decade. The backing vocals—Bobby Bird's *Yeah!* and James Brown's *Whoo!*—provide a soundtrack for these tunes, which usually feature an artist like Madonna, a woman singing about a relationship. You may have noticed a refrain by now, the multiple cameos, directly or indirectly, that

James Brown and "funky" make on *Erotica*. Just to drive home the debt, the final track of *Erotica*, "Secret Garden," takes one final sample from the Godfather of Soul, in this case his "Soul Pride." He's been the patron saint of the album the whole way through.

And yet there is a specific, even if probably unintentional, thematic echo in the lyrics of "Think (About it)" and "Bye Bye Baby." Both are about a woman reflecting on a midpoint in a relationship, deciding whether it is worth continuing. Collins: *Those of you who go out and stay out all night and half the next day and expect us to be home when you get there. But let me tell you something. The sisters are not going for that no more.* Madonna: *I keep on waiting, anticipating, but I can't wait forever. . . . You had your chances, all your romances, and now I just don't want you.* Like the songs she samples, Madonna knows not just how to make the erotic but how to end it, how to turn off the lights and kill the mood. *This is not a love song*, Madonna begins this track, and the *whoo! yeah!* backdrop gives an ironically enthusiastic assent: men whose voices seem distant, already gone, but agreeing.

3. The Erotic Needs an Exotic, Nostalgic Soundtrack to Get You in the Mood.

This may not seem that sexy at first: the interpolation of *Sound of Music*'s "Do-Re-Mi" in "Deeper and Deeper." Why is Madonna borrowing the lyrics from the song in which Julie Andrews teaches her young Austrian charges how to sing, on the brink of war? When Madonna sings, *When you know the notes to sing, you can sing most anything: that's what my mama told me*, she's lifting the first two lines from the Rodgers and Hammerstein musical, which makes Julie Andrews her mama (in fact, real mother Madonna Louise Ciccone was born just two years before Julie Andrews). What's interesting is what comes next in this opening verse: *'Round and 'round and 'round you go; when you find love, you'll always know.* These lyrics suggest the trials of dating, the repetition and recycling of partners on the way to the "love" who is presumably the one—an endpoint to what is otherwise a rotating circle.

By pairing the beginning of song with the beginning of dating, Madonna's appropriation of the musical's lyrics recasts the project of her musical career as a whole, suggesting that each song, just as it is a rearrangement of the fundamental notes *do-re-mi*, is also a rearrangement of different fundamental experiences in love. That this song begins in its first verse with this singing lesson also suggests how much, for Madonna, the fundamental experiences are already borrowed—already taught or filtered through the songs that came before, just as her mother came before her in love.

And, of course, *Erotica* would not be what it is if Madonna didn't borrow from herself, too, especially in the sampling of "Vogue" in *Erotica*'s "Deeper and Deeper." As you can tell, this track is Madonna's most eclectic and sample-heavy on the album. The movement through different soundscapes suggests the movement of love itself: the constant search Madonna tells us about in the lyrics, looking for the one who will make it so her *love is alive*. We started off with a lesson from a governess, then learned from flamenco how to grow up out of childhood, and now, in the song's final moments, we don't have to learn from anyone else except from Madonna herself. She interpolates lyrics from her "Vogue" in the song's outro: *You've got to just let your body go with the flow* is now sandwiched between the added lyrics of *Never gonna have to pretend*. It's funny, since vogueing is all about pretending: *Strike a pose, there's nothing to it.* And so, too, does the invocation to *let your body go* make it sound like this singer hasn't been in love after all—that the repeated declaration she *can't help falling in love* might just be overcompensation for not feeling the love at all. It's music, not the lover, that will make you fall in love. That's the lesson of the samples from this song: you start with music to start your love life, you turn to flamenco to make it hotter, and no matter what, you can always, ultimately, count on Madonna to give you *the flow* to *let your body go.*

3
Madonna/Whore

"In the record business, 1992 may well be remembered as the year of the $100 million superstar deal," noted Michael Goldberg in the first issue of *Rolling Stone* in 1993.[1] The headliner was Prince, but notable mentions went to Elton John, ZZ Top, and, of course, Madonna, who had signed a deal worth about $50 million with Time Warner. The deal was multimedia and wide-ranging, as Goldberg had also reported with insider information when it was made toward the end of the previous spring: Madonna

> has made separate deals for recording, song publishing and film and TV production, as well as the formation of a new record label. . . . Time Warner will produce her HBO concert specials (for which Madonna will receive between $1 million and $2 million each) but is under no obligation to produce other film or TV projects she presents to the company. Her new record label, a joint venture with Time

[1] Michael Goldberg, "The Art of the Deal," *Rolling Stone*, no. 647 (January 7, 1993).

Warner, . . . will provide $3 million to $5 million a year for a minimum of three years to cover overhead, artist advances and recording costs.[2]

The record label was called Maverick—taking a syllable each from the first names of its cofounders: Madonna, Veronica "Ronnie" Dashev, and Frederick DeMann (Madonna's manager)—and within a decade it would sign artists ranging from Alanis Morissette to Muse and Paul Oakenfold. But its first productions were Madonna's *Sex*, the book, and *Erotica*, the album.

Erotica is the album and 1992 is the year that announced Madonna had arrived not only as an entertainer but also as an entertainment mogul. Throughout the 1990s, she was one of the only women in the music business with her own label. And to launch that business with *Sex* was to confirm something people often whispered, usually loudly, about her: that she was a sex worker, someone who sold sex. This Madonna was a whore.

When Sigmund Freud, the father of psychoanalysis, identified the Madonna-whore complex in the early 1900s, he was talking not about women but about a problem men had with women. Dividing all of women into two mutually exclusive categories, the saintly Madonnas and the slutty sex workers, was the projection of a split inside men themselves, who had tried to bifurcate love and desire. "The whole sphere of love in such persons remains divided in the two directions

---

[2]Michael Goldberg, "Madonna to Sign $60 Million Deal," *Rolling Stone*, no. 628 (April 16, 1992).

personified in art as sacred and profane (or animal) love," he wrote.[3] Ironically, Madonna herself has often tried to maintain a border between the sexual and the romantic. The very first sentences on the very first page of *Sex* announce: "This book is about sex. Sex is not love. Love is not sex." But to call some women whores was a man's way to disavow his own deep-seated feelings of lust, his own sexuality he felt was degrading and degraded. To be able to sequester this part of himself through the fantasy of sequestering all the whores in the world was a way to preserve the hope that there could be a pure love untainted by sexuality itself—a spirituality that transcended the physical.

But the whore is the opposite of the Madonna not just because the whore is sexual and the Madonna is virginal, not yet *touched for the very first time*. The whore is also opposite from the Madonna because she's into sex not for the sex but for the money. And this, too, requires separating something like love from sex, to make it business rather than lust, professional rather than personal. In *Sex*, Madonna similarly seems to be able to turn the sexual on and off to make a buck.

As the cultural critic Karlene Faith has observed, Madonna "came out as the antithesis of the socially committed 'folk madonnas' of the sixties, epitomized by the three Js—Joan

[3]See Sigmund Freud, "On the Universal Tendency to Debasement in the Sphere of Love (Contributions to the Psychology of Love II)," in *The Standard Edition of the Complete Psychological Works of Sigmund Freud*, ed. James Strachey, vol. 11 (London: Hogarth, 1957), 177–90.

Baez, Joni Mitchell, and Judy Collins."[4] Madonna embraced and reclaimed an identity as "a refreshingly proud Whore in the Mae West tradition," one who accepts the epithet as a sign that men fear the power she has over her own body. She has said of Eva Peron, whom she would play in *Evita* in 1996 and who was herself accused of sleeping to the top of Argentine politics, that

> the aristocrats and most men . . . were completely frightened by the kind of power that she had. And it's always easy, it's the most obvious and predictable way out, to call a woman a whore and imply that she has no morals and no integrity and no talent. And God knows, I can relate to that. It's the oldest trick in the book.[5]

What her analysis picks up on is that what men are really afraid of is not so much the whore's sexual promiscuity but the whore's sexual business: she has found a way to make an income in an economy that is supposed to bar women as a class. An early profile from the November 22, 1984, issue of *Rolling Stone* noted that Madonna turned on the sex appeal at the most economic moments: "This is a woman who saves her sex-bomb act for when the meter's running."[6]

---

[4]Karlene Faith, *Madonna, Bawdy and Soul* (Toronto, ON: University of Toronto Press, 1997), 41.

[5]Quoted in ibid., 36.

[6]Christopher Connely, "Madonna Goes All the Way," *Rolling Stone*, no. 435 (November 22, 1984).

Madonna is a whore, proudly, because she is a business-woman. She had proudly announced her desire to enter into that identity a couple of years before *Erotica*, in the famous, because famously canceled, commercial she made for Pepsi. The commercial aired once in the United States, during a March 2, 1989, episode of *The Cosby Show*, and 250 million people across the world tuned in after being promised the two-minute spot was also going to premiere Madonna's new single, "Like a Prayer," which was officially released along with a music video on MTV the following day. The commercial features Madonna watching home videos, ultimately telling a birthday girl in one to make a wish. But the official music video leaned more heavily into the song's blasphemy, its innuendos about being *down on my knees, I wanna take you there, in the midnight hour I can feel your power*. For instance, she makes out with a saint in a church. Viewers, conflating the two videos, boycotted Pepsi, which pulled the commercial.

The incident is telling for how it brought together the emerging side of business, which is the subject of this chapter, with Madonna's persistent relation of appropriating politics, which was the subject of the previous chapter. Madonna said of the commercial, right before it aired:

> I like the challenge of merging art and commerce. As far as I'm concerned, making a video is also a commercial. But the treatment for the video is a lot more controversial. It's probably going to touch a lot of nerves in a lot of people. And the treatment for the commercial is . . . I mean, it's a commercial. It's very, very sweet. It's very sentimental. The Pepsi spot is a great and different way to expose the

record. Record companies just don't have the money to finance that kind of publicity.[7]

Madonna had become an expert at a kind of synergy, a multi-commodity integration, hustling one item through hustling another, always having the next hustle in mind.

In this hustle, Madonna turned to ambiguous political imagery to meet the "challenge of merging art and commerce." In the MTV music video, that saint Madonna makes out with is Black. Later, after a white police officer arrests a Black man falsely accused of the murder of a white man, Madonna is seen dancing in a field at night, KKK crosses burning in the background. In the official story that the video's visuals, rather than the song's lyrics, seem to be telling, Madonna is at the church to get the courage to testify in defense of the arrestee, since Madonna has seen the white mob actually responsible for the murder. This shocking imagery aims to elevate the "commerce" of the video into "art," in the way she thought Mapplethorpe's style might elevate the content of *Sex*, as explored in the previous chapter. Blackness and racism are often on standby for Madonna's purposes, helping to bridge the sacred and the religious, the artistic and the commercial.

In his contribution to *The Madonna Connection*, the edited volume of academic essays on Madonna as a cultural phenomenon that was released the same year as *Erotica*, Ronald B. Scott noted that, amid the racial polarization suggested by burning crosses, Madonna "challenges

[7]Zehme, "Madonna: The *Rolling Stone* Interview."

viewers not by advocating interracial relationships but by presenting images that confront them with their own historically grounded prejudice."[8] In this more optimistic reading, Madonna does not offer a magical solution to racism through romance, but instead confronts just how thorough of a problem racism is, something that individual choice cannot destroy. Instead, intervention at a structural level is needed: not just the bad things individuals think but the bad outcomes produced by social inequality, economic opportunity, and governmental neglect. Scott is particularly interested in Madonna's relation to the Black Church, not just for the gospel sounds she appropriates but for its own institutional strength as "a viable force in the worldly concerns of blacks," because "it has been able to successfully fuse the secular and sacred concerns into a viable working philosophy that touches the lives of virtually every member of the black community."[9] From this view, what may seem sacrilegious may also be respect for the specificity of religion in Black communities. "Instead of sacrilege, the specific images of burning crosses behind Madonna are symbolically both a reminder of the political and social extremes of racism and a tribute to the steadfast and salutatory role the black church has historically played in providing a safe haven from

[8] Ronald B. Scott, "Images of Race and Religion in Madonna's Video Like a Prayer: Prayer and Praise," in *The Madonna Connection: Representational Politics, Subcultural Identities, and Cultural Theory*, ed. Cathy Schwichtenberg (Boulder, CO: Westview Press, 1993), 67.

[9] Ibid., 69.

the racist assaults that have threatened blacks throughout their history in this country."[10]

At the same time, it matters that Madonna's message is ambiguous precisely because of the diversity of an audience that could code the same images as belonging to more than one tradition and more than one political inspiration. The ambiguity of the video's message is also a sales strategy. In *Erotica*, songs and music videos take on such a range of references and influences that single meanings are hard to peg down, opening them up for more interpretation, more confusion—and so more need to be talked about, discussed, bought, and sold.

It was a formula that often worked. In 1990, *Forbes*, estimating Madonna had made more than $125 million in the previous five years, put her on their cover with pink trim around the border to match her pink velvet outfit with sparkling dollar-sign buttons; in all caps, the title read, "AMERICA'S SMARTEST BUSINESS WOMAN?" It was design and the limitations of space that forced a line break between business and woman, but the split is still meaningful: Is Madonna a business or a businesswoman? Long before it became trendy for individuals to talk of having their own "brand"—a professional identity, a personality become a commodity—Madonna had been straddling the divide between being a business and being a woman, being a brand and being a person. This is the second sense in which Madonna is, proudly, a whore, for what she makes money

[10]Ibid., 71.

off of is not just the "public" goods put in the market as albums, promotional materials, and concert tickets but also her own "private" self, offering not so much sex but a sex life, captured in the tabloid reportage on her public boyfriends. By the time of *Erotica*, the roster included, in addition to her first marriage to Sean Penn, Basquiat (she was turned off by his drug use), Dennis Rodman (who was reportedly selfish in bed and overcompensated in his tell-all memoir by claiming Madonna was a whore), and, ever styling herself in the image of Marilyn Monroe, a Kennedy. She couldn't sing *Happy Birthday, Mr. President*, but settled for his son, JFK, Jr.

What the cliché of sex work as "the oldest profession in the world" tacitly acknowledges is that sex work has always been at the avant-garde of work itself. This has continued to be the case under the recent period of political economic history sometimes called "neoliberalism." In the past fifty years, many of the social benefits and public resources founded in the aftermath of the Great Depression have been hollowed out, which means workers must fend for themselves. Rapidly declining tax rates for the rich have effectively redistributed wealth upwards, leading to the greatest wealth gap in the history of the United States. And the workers who continue to work in this landscape of exploitation must now work all the time to make ends meet, from the part-time cashier at Target who must Uber on the side to the office worker who answers emails at 10:00 p.m. at night when they're supposed to be "off" watching TV on the couch. A nine-to-five job is a luxury these days; the luxury is having a clearly marked end to a workday. Now, everyone has to hustle, has to work like a hustler.

In the 1990s, Madonna not only performed as a singer but also performed working itself. In the book accompanying *The Girlie Show*, the tour that brought *Erotica*'s music to the stage in 1993, she reflected on her previous tour from 1990:

> When I finished the *Blond Ambition* tour, I swore on my life that I would never even think of going on tour again as long as I lived. I was spent. I was exhausted. I was sick of traveling. I wanted stability. So, I threw myself into making movies, recording a new album, and I also put out a book called *Sex*. So much for stability.

Instability, constantly working, working one's self sick: these are the traits Madonna shares, at least in name, with other neoliberal workers.

A background story to this emerging work-all-the-time situation is a change in the kinds of labor demanded by the current economy. In a previous period of industrialization, the main scene of labor was a factory, which often had clearly marked times to clock in and clock out. Moreover, workers concentrated in the same physical workplace made it easier to unionize, forming collective bargaining units that could protect worker rights and working conditions. In the late twentieth century, however, rapid deindustrialization led to a concentration of labor in a different kind of work: the service sector. Whether in retail or waiting tables, this kind of service is different in many key ways. For one, hours may be less regular. For another, this work often includes not producing or making a commodity but instead what the sociologist Arlie Hochschild has called the "emotional labor" of selling a commodity: making a customer feel good, smiling—being, in a way, seductive.[11] For this reason, service labor has often been feminized, considered "women's work" and therefore deserving of lower wages.

Perhaps the greatest difference from factory work is how service workers get paid this lower wage. Rather than a secure or regular salary, many in the service industry are paid in tips, which means their compensation is not actually coming from their employer or the restaurant they work at but from the customers themselves. The tip economy is one of the ways in which bosses have artificially increased their own profits, because it allows them to pay their workers' subminimum wages with the expectation that customer tips will lift the wage above minimum. Workers have no guaranteed wage; they must depend on leaving a good impression on their customers. Moreover, it is hard for these workers to organize for a better deal. Unlike the production and manufacturing sectors that provided the central scenes of strike actions in the classic labor movement, the service sector is radically segmented, stymying collective action. The same can be said of the gig economy or the share economy, with Uber drivers, for instance, finding it both difficult to unionize and reliant upon their riders for the tips that make the ends meet.

Sex work is at the avant-garde of this economy, because it has usually included the conditions of labor involved in the kinds of entrepreneurial and service labor that have become generalized under neoliberalism and deindustrialization. First, a whore is in business for herself, an entrepreneur who

[11]Arlie Russell Hochschild, *The Managed Heart: Commercialization of Human Feeling* (Berkeley, CA: University of California Press, 1983).

sells her brand rather than working for a company. Second, a whore makes as much money as her customers are willing to pay or tip for her services. Third, a whore lacks the labor protections of an established workplace, not to mention a union. And a whore does not work set hours, clocking in and out of the factory, but rather works in an on-demand fashion, always on call, always a "call girl."

Madonna had first flirted with the imagery and tropes of sex work in her music video for "Open Your Heart" from her 1986 *True Blue* album, her third studio album. Directed by Jean Baptiste Mondino (who would later return for the "Justify My Love" music video as well), the video features Madonna on stage alone at a *Cabaret*-style peep show (she starts off in a fringy, black Liza Minelli wig). The slots through which her customers watch the show are stylized to look like television screens. In some shots, the live customers have been replaced with wooden cut-outs of Art Deco paintings by Tamara de Lempicka; a reproduction of the painter's work featuring three nude women also provides the signage for the peep show establishment as a whole. Madonna is a collector of Lempicka's work, which would reappear in the videos for "Express Yourself" and "Vogue" as well as the stage sets for the *Who's That Girl* and *Blond Ambition* tours. In this video, their two-dimensional prop nature works to remind us we are on a clearly artificial and stylized stage—a stage that has obviously been built for the single purpose of being the set for this music video.

This fantasy of sex work invites historical confusion, or rather, an intentionally promiscuous play with multiple historical periods: 1920s Berlin, in which *Cabaret* is set;

1960s Broadway, in which the play was first produced; 1970s Hollywood, where the Minelli film adaptation was shot; and the present day, in which some of Madonna's customers come dressed in stock broker suits. The oldest profession is the longest lasting profession, and Madonna suggests a persistence to the basic facts of sex work. At the same time, the "show" of the peep show has migrated mediums. She is performing live in this video, but in a way that references television and Hollywood, and, of course, in a way that reminds us that this, too, is another medium and genre: the music video itself. In turn, she suggests how mediated something like sex, or pornography, has become. Peep shows have always been set up to bar physical access between a customer and a dancer, but now there are even more barriers: the distance of Hollywood, the distance of MTV. This is not a loss but a way in which sex can take over more and more frontiers, can make more and more business even as the basic facts of sex remain pretty much the same.

If you were a young queer kid watching this music video, you would probably remember, more than Madonna's dance, her customers. In one peeping booth, we see a woman, a nod to same-sex attraction. In another booth, we see two Navy men on leave: officially heterosexual, but noticeably in the same booth, as if Madonna might just be triangulating their own same-sex desire (they are holding hands). This is reminiscent of Gene Kelly and Frank Sinatra in *Anchors Aweigh*, as I explored in Chapter 1. Take Madonna out of the picture, and you've still got two guys in one booth. But, most controversially and memorably, there is the potential customer who never makes it into the show: the child actor and model Felix Howard. Before we see Madonna on stage, we see him outside the theater, trying to buy a ticket but fooling no one about his age, even if dressed in suit and hat. Intercut throughout the video are shots of Howard admiring, or rather studying, the posters on the theater walls. In a mirror, he starts miming what he imagines are Madonna's moves. At the end, Madonna comes out and kisses him gently on the lips. They are now dressed alike, in loose-fitting gray suits with the same short, prickly blonde hair, and they run off, dancing, into the sunrise. The theater owner had misread the boy's intentions: he did not want to see Madonna but to *be* Madonna.

There was the expected conservative backlash to this video and its intergenerational, if chaste, kiss. But to me, this video is less about sex and more about gender identity; and, to me, Howard is less a horny straight teenager than, perhaps, a trans teenager. What seems important is how performance makes possible this connection between Madonna and Howard, and this performance in particular of sex. Sex work provides a scene for identification, fantasy, projection, and community for the queer outside to this show. It provides a scene for what the English literature scholar Alexander Eastwood calls "reading for resonance." Eastwood approaches literature from the perspective of a trans person who is hungry for finding representations of trans people in the past but is likely to be disappointed by "mimesis," a narration of the lives of people who were plausibly trans. When reading a text that "contains no identifiable trans characters," Eastwood instead looks for what he calls "resonance," a term associated with sound that he borrows from literary critic Wai Chee Dimock's own use of it in the context of reading; as Dimock says, "A text can be read only insofar as readers manage to inflect it. And, in hanging so perilously on that inflection, it tunes the ear to what eludes the eye, what is not optically evident from the typographic marks on the page."[12] For Eastwood, this means inflecting a text that is not overtly trans with trans themes and experiences: "in providing representations of transsexuality that exceed narrative identification, they equip the contemporary reader with methods for reading the latent presence of trans affects, temporalities, and bodies in more canonical and historical texts."[13] For instance, the anxious experience of coming out, or the shaming experience of hiding a part of one's self, or the disorienting experience of seeing one's pre-transition self as both similar and dissimilar from who one is today: these experiences of emotions and time are trans in their nature, even if not embodied in obviously trans characters.

This is the trans resonance to a song like "Open Your Heart." In other words, besides what the horny stock brokers are getting out of Madonna's striptease, Madonna herself and unintended audience members like Howard are getting something else out of it, forging their own meanings. Some feminists read the ending of the music video, Madonna dancing down the street with the child, as an escape from

[12]Wai Chee Dimock, "A Theory of Resonance," *PMLA: Publications of the Modern Language Association of America* 112, no. 5 (1997): 1066.

[13]Alexander Eastwood, "How, Then, Might the Transsexual Read?: Notes toward a Trans Literary History," *TSQ: Transgender Studies Quarterly* 1, no. 4 (2014): 601.

sex work, fleeing the handsy guys and becoming no longer a prostitute but more like a mother. For some feminists, this is empowering, abandoning the patriarchal gaze. But this interpretation misses what makes Madonna's sex work so surprising in this video. First of all, Madonna has one of the cushiest and safest gigs as a sex worker: indoor work, with physical barriers between her and customers. But second, she controls the meanings that her work produces, as well as the kinds of community those meanings make possible. This is the cultural avant-garde of sex work, its improvisation of new kinds of community and identification. It makes itself available for different resonances, just as song itself can be remixed into different sonic territory.

* * *

The most unusual song on *Erotica*—and only available on the uncensored album—is more about Madonna than by her. It's a rap track on which Andre Betts, Mark Goodman, and Dave Murphy talk about whether Betts fucked Madonna in her limo. Arriving right after the AIDS elegy "In This Life," the subject matter is particularly jarring. "Did You Do It?" is mostly a joke track, not unlike the final song on Madonna's last studio album, "Act of Contrition," a noisy recording that began with Madonna improvising lyrics—mostly failing, as a lapsed Catholic, to remember the words to the prayer that shares the name of the song itself: *O my God, I am heartily sorry for having offended Thee, and I detest all my sins, because I dread the loss of heaven, and the pains of hell*—on top of the music from "Like a Prayer" playing backwards. There is a mirror symmetry here: "Like a Prayer" was the first track on this album with which it shares a name, and now Madonna is closing out the religious theme by intentionally making it sacrilegious. Aspiring Satanists have dissected the song for subliminal messages in the noise, but all that is worth finding here is the apocalyptic guitar solo provided by Prince, with whom Madonna had a brief affair.

"Did You Do It?" is like "Act of Contrition" not just because of its serious unseriousness but because it, too, uses another Madonna track as a foundation upon which another man makes his mark. If Prince played atop "Like a Prayer" in the earlier song, while Madonna improvised, in this song from *Erotica* Betts is extemporaneously rapping atop the beat from Madonna's "Waiting," with a sample of Madonna's voice occasionally breaking through: *Waiting for you, just waiting. Waiting for you.* Betts had previously coproduced, with Lenny Kravitz, Madonna's "Justify My Love," which is a kind of godmother to *Erotica* as a whole, its aspirational steaminess and its spoken word lyrics. As a producer for both, Betts is selling Madonna's sound, but in "Did You Do It?" he is also selling his own sound, this time using Madonna's body as a means: the gossip over whether or not they fucked.

It is tempting to call this—selling Madonna's sex life and sound—a relation of pimping, but only because sex work is directly mentioned in the song's lyrics, especially in the second verse, when the scene shifts from a limo going around Central Park to a sex worker receiving a call from *your John* and then meeting him while he's wearing a *pamper and a fur coat*. What's noticeable is how quickly the scene has changed, as well as the type of sex and work involved.

The stereotypical *pamper and fur coat* invokes a New York City pimp from 1970s Blaxploitation films, and Betts seems to be riding the late 1980s trend of rapping about pimping led by Ice-T's 1987 "Somebody Gotta Do It (Pimpin' Ain't Easy!!!)." But *your John* is slang for a sex worker's client, not a pimp. There are other inconsistencies, too. Notably, the sex worker in this verse seems at first to be a street-based worker, soliciting clients as they drive by her stroll: *Walkin' around showing off their hinies*. But then the worker is a call girl, someone less likely to be working the street because her customers make an appointment through the telephone: *Yo Ho, your phone's ringin'*. This verse is a grab bag of sex worker tropes and lingo, without really narrating or describing a single, coherent sex worker.

In any case, this composite image of *an average Ho* is, clearly, no longer Madonna, who would never sign off on a lyric on her album calling her *average*. The picture is clarified in the remainder of the verse, in which Betts explains *I dipped it and I stripped it and I ripped it like before*. The line *I dipped it and I tripped it and I ripped it* uncannily anticipates the 1996 interactive children's toy that will call out for players to *twist it and pop it and bop it*. But these silly lyrics hide what also seems to be a scene of sexual violence as Betts continues over protestation: *nope no diddily, nope no more, I can't stop once I get started*. What is most telling in these lines, though, is the transition from working on the streets to the odd domesticity of Betts's home where this sex worker becomes *like Campbell's soup*, an opportunity to allude to eating her out. Another joke track earlier on the album goes for almost six full minutes (!) extending the metaphor of *Dining in and eating out* and the reminder that *Dining out can happen down below: Now what could be better than a home cooked meal.* That song, in its least sexy moment, turns Madonna's pussy into a KFC drive-through: *Colonel Sanders says it best, Finger lickin' good.*

The connotations of Campbell's soup are a little different. It is the American mass-produced commodity bar none, made famous for its sterile ubiquity by Andy Warhol's screen prints, but it is also what your mother makes you when you're sick—which only suggests how much family life, too, has become mass-produced, fed, and maintained by a steady diet of industrial production. Sex work often provides a scene in which questions of the repetitive and sterile meet the hot and unique. From the perspective of work, a trick is just another trick, a John is just another John, and a sex act purchased is just like any sex act purchased, like a can of Campbell's soup. But from the perspective of sex, a trick is supposed to be better than the rote masturbation Betts references with *Peter was on the beater.* Sex is supposed to be a good time, but purchasing it is also just purchasing time itself, sold in one-hour increments.

When Betts says this is just *another episode* and that *It ain't all about working on the streets no more*, he is suggesting how much he thinks this boring nature of work—buying time, selling another commodity—has become characteristic of exchanges and activities beyond sex work, including his own work of producing and remixing and sampling tracks. Like sex, a single is supposed to be hot, but it's also supposed to be, like Campbell's soup, a bit familiar: a beat somewhat recognizable that you would know what to do with when it came over the radio. Neither pop nor dance are supposed to be too experimental, at the same time that they must keep staying somewhat new, somehow fresh—surprising but not too surprising. It's a hustle to negotiate this balance.

The stress of this negotiation is evident in the sound of this song. The rap, of course, is where it starts. It's a dramatic upgrade from the other innovation of this album, which is Madonna's decision to speak rather than sing many of her lyrics, including the *waiting for you* that repeats throughout this particular track. But as if anxious that rap is not itself enough of an update, the song ends up flailing, searching for more influence or inspiration. The third verse, in turn, is suddenly, unnecessarily, reggae, with Betts affecting a Jamaican accent: *Clean up me rifle, elephant rifle.* We've heard reggae influences before, as I addressed in the previous chapter of this book: the way it facilitated the color-blind dream of all the *brothers and sisters* coming together in "Why's It So Hard." In this particular song of *Erotica*, however, the rapper seems restless to even stay in Jamaica, choosing as his metaphor for his big dick an image from an African safari: *me elephant rifle.* What a world tour we've taken, even as it's been miniaturized in the trip from the street to the call booth to the apartment kitchen.

*   *   *

The rapid movement through different sonic landscapes in the sex work anthem of *Erotica* suggests the extent to which Madonna and her producers understood their own work of pimping sound as a kind of hustling, the need to keep finding new and different sounds to make the next one-night-stand feel different than just a one-night-stand. This is the difficult task of keeping sex interesting, of dressing up a finite set of actions with some hornier garb, of extending the mood beyond the most recent orgasm. And, in *Erotica*, this kind of sex work, work to keep sex sexy, comes in its sound effects. When the melody gets strained, when the chorus has been repeated one too many times without any improvisation, you can always bring in a sound effect for surprise, for mood, for action. An annotated list of *Erotica*'s sound effects:

1. The opening static in "Erotica." Before this album even properly begins, or rather what is the proper beginning of this album, there is some vinyl crackling on the opening and title track. It sets the tone, before Madonna even introduces her alter ego: *My name is Dita, I'll be your mistress tonight. I'd like to put you in a trance*. Dita, a professional dominatrix, has something to sell, but the album is already selling her as a sex worker from the sexy yesteryear, the retro years of interwar cabaret. Madonna says she named her alter ego after Dita Parlo, the German film actress most active in the 1930s, but on stage she draws as much from Marlene Dietrich, who got her start as the cabaret singer Lola Lola, who brings about a professor's descent from respectability in Josef von Sternberg's *The Blue Angel* (1930).

The vinyl crackling on a cassette or CD indicates the lack of eroticism at the cutting edge of technology. Vinyl is more tactile—you can feel the crackle in a way you can't feel a CD skip. There is also something more intimate about the physical object of the record, something that, even if mass-produced, feels more singular than a cassette bought off a rack stuffed full of them. The irony is that what provides the foundation for most of *Erotica*'s tracks is digital technology: synth drums, samples processed through a sample machine. The opening crackle also reminds us how much we aren't listening to a record, how much a sense of tactile intimacy must be faked rather than enjoyed. But this is what eroticism often amounts to: a longing for what we don't have. Of course, a cassette wants a record—either to be or to have.

But what is it we long for but don't have? Is it the past represented by an older technology? Is it the sense of touch represented by the feel of a record's grooves? Is it the monogamy represented by the singularity of the physical record, like a photograph versus its promiscuous digital copy? Whatever it is we desire, Madonna's Dita is here to sell it to us.

2. Snapped fingers in "Fever." This song is rare in Madonna's oeuvre because it's a cover and a cover that continues to speak Madonna's desire for the femmes of yesteryear. The iconic recording of the song, Peggy Lee's in 1958, was itself a cover, too. Its original singer was R&B artist Little Willie John, whose difference in race and gender from both Madonna and Peggy Lee also complicates the song's meanings. It was in the Lee recording that extra verses about history's feverous were added, notably Romeo and Juliet and Captain Smith and Pocahontas: *Fever isn't such a new thing, Fever started long ago.* The song is in line with Madonna's own sense that to find the erotic, you have to keep going back in time. But notably, these stores are also both fictional: the fiction of playwright Shakespeare, in the first case, and the fiction of an accumulated history of gossip, in the second case. Pocahontas was real, but the love story of a colonist and colonized is, historians largely agree, embellished. And these stories are, each in their way, tragic. The dual suicide of Romeo and Juliet or, you know, the colonizing.

That the go-to characters for a story about being overcome by a love fever are star-crossed lovers who die suggests a larger mythology about love: that you're supposed to want to die for it, that death is even the measure of a love's strength, just as a passionate flame must all the more quickly go out. In the context of AIDS—in the context of a sexual fever that really could kill you—this is, as I explored in Chapter 1, tricky territory. *You give me fever*, but a fever is exactly what you don't want from a sexual partner. And yet the historical distance seems to make this territory easier to navigate. Handed down through generations of myth-making, Juliet and Pocahontas do not immediately make most listeners think of tragedy, even if they are tragic. And the 1950s sound of "Fever" itself might, for a listener in the 1990s, provide a sense of desexualization, too: teenagers think of their parents wearing poodle skirts.

But it is the persistence of the chorus of snapped fingers that really does make this song work, whether in Peggy Lee's cover or in Madonna's. They bring to mind a smoky lounge, which is sexy. But they also bring to mind something folksy, which is probably not as sexy. Most importantly, they remind us that a singer is on a stage, that there is indeed a choir rather than an intimate duet. This is a singer telling her friends about fever, rather than having a fever in the moment. What

Madonna is selling us is the promise of fever, rather than its performance. By keeping the erotic always just off stage, somewhere in the past or somewhere in the wings, we can keep anticipating, keep signing up for the tease.

3. Record scratching in "Bye Bye Baby." As a transition between verses on this track, you can hear a little scratching of an album on a turntable. This is a progression from the crackling on the opening track. Now, we're not listening to something old but something new: a DJ on the dance floor, scrubbing their records. This is how this third song on the album tries to get us rapidly into the present, after the 1930s Germany of "Erotica" or the 1950s United States of "Fever." And there's a notably lyrical explanation the song provides on more than one occasion of self-labeling: *This is not a love song.* Record scratching means we're on the dance floor, and you don't go to the dance floor looking for love.

What matters is that by showing this range, this jumping of times and places, Madonna cements her status as the MC, the ringleader, our guide. She is the one constant. The sound effects give us a sense of her position as our Dita, who will sell us the possibility of fever and the rejection of love.

4. Bleeping out the end of "Bye Bye Baby." The F-word is bleeped out in the final verse: *You can forget about it baby, 'cause it's the first time and the last time you'll ever see me cry. You f***ed it up.* Just as record scratching tells us we're on the dance floor, this censorship suggests we're on the radio or even television. A couple of years later, Madonna will have a notorious visit to the *Late Show with David Letterman*, where she'll say "fuck" fourteen times—then the record for the most words needing censorship on a single episode of a talk show. We've moved to a more public scene, and publics have more rules.

By invoking another medium, Madonna also sells herself as a multi-platform artist. She was always an aspiring actress, of course, something she did not receive acclaim for until *Evita* in 1996. But most importantly, she always sold her projects as bundles. In 1992, there was the bundle of the book *Sex*, the album *Erotica*, and the film *Body of Evidence*. What is most telling about bleeping out fuck is that, on this particular medium, an album that bears a Parental Advisory label, she doesn't need to bleep out fuck. Madonna wants the censorship more than the thing being censored; wants the performance of breaking a rule more than the pleasure of the breaking itself. What she is selling *is* the Parental Advisory label, the seduction of doing something your parents advise against, something naughty. She knows we don't want to buy porn or rather that's not what we want to buy with this album. We want the black bars covering genitals, want the bleeping out of fuck. It's hotter the more things are almost, but not yet, laid bare. The tease rather than the fuck.

5. Glass breaking, gum smacking, and sirens wailing in "Thief of Hearts." This song takes its title a little too seriously. It's Madonna's "Jolene," about a woman who has stolen her man's heart and his paternity: *Little miss thinks she can have his child.* In the year leading up to *Erotica*'s release, two of Madonna's highest-profile exes had indeed had their first children with other women: Sean Penn with

Robin Wright in 1991; Warren Beatty with Annette Benning in 1992. But the theatricality of making a metaphoric theft sound like a real one—a breaking and entering, the police coming—also makes it feel less personal, which is perhaps how most things are with Madonna and why her allure is different from a Dolly Parton, whose celebrity is more often built on the warmth of her personality and the cuteness of her low-profile, loving marriage to the same man since 1966.

This is, furthermore, a theatricality Madonna has learned from the movie she made with Warren Beatty: the crime comedy flick *Dick Tracy*. In her discography, the first time we encounter the sound effect of glass shattering is in the songs she contributed to the movie's soundtrack. In "Now I'm Following You (Part II)" on that soundtrack, Madonna plays with sound effects to great effect: the song about dancing with her lover begins with the record skipping a beat, and by the end, the record gets stuck stuttering on the character's first name: *Dick, dick, dick, dick.* (Madonna quips: *My bottom hurts just thinking about it.*) The scratching and crackling sound effects on *Erotica* are more sophisticated, not played for laughs but more for sensuality, and yet they retain the sense of fun that Madonna seems to have had on the movie soundtrack.

Making her love triangle sound like a crime flick is not just Madonna re-announcing her prolonged ambition to be a movie star. It's also her way of selling love itself as a performance, as a movie flick: her relationships with movie stars, whether Penn or Beatty, are themselves made cinematic in this song about thievery. It's like she's saying not to take things too seriously. But in the gum smacking that comes after the breaking glass, we also get a sense of her being the femme fatale in the end, not the victim of thievery but the boss standing over the scene, coolly chewing gum in the way a noir detective of a previous age smoked a long cigarette. If anyone is the mob boss, Madonna says, it's Madonna. Victimhood doesn't long suit her.

6. Typewriter clacking at the end of "Words." What a sonic roller coaster is this song: a serene orchestral beginning gets jumpy, and then catchy, leading us through some lyrics that are about how much words hurt before landing us on the sound effect of a machine that prints them: a typewriter. The second-person address of the song—*You try to humiliate with your words*—invokes an intimate relationship, but the song really seems addressed to the media, whether the tabloids that might have covered a relationship with Penn or Beatty, or the popular critic that more recently, in the age of social media-facilitated verbal abuse, we have come to call a troll. In 1994, two years after *Erotica*, St. Martin's Press would publish *The I Hate Madonna Handbook*, which included a scrapbook of her least fine moments. The back cover invites: "Do you hate Madonna and don't know why? Would you like to hate Madonna but don't have the tools? At last, here's everything you need to justify the feeling you get whenever the Hype Priestess crosses your screen. Not just for card-carrying Madonna haters, this book is for all the fence-sitters who ever wondered: Just who is this undressed woman, and why won't she leave us alone? Consisting of ten stinging chapters, each guaranteed to make you scream with delight and disbelief, this is the therapeutic read you've been waiting for. Who knew hating Madonna could be this much fun?"

Like the analog status of vinyl scratches on this digital album, a typewriter is also a historical throwback. The 1990s is the opening age of the personal computer, not the clunky typewriter. By the time of *Erotica*, AOL was beginning to introduce personal email addresses, leading to the ubiquitous robotic soundbite: *You've got mail.* The internet, too, transformed the landscape and nature of sex work, in part by providing different ways of selling and acquiring it. Personal escort pages, adult chat rooms: all from the comfort of your own home, if you could afford a computer. This is sex work without a middleman, or at least, not a middle*man*: more like the intermediary of an internet company, an anonymous multinational organization who knew you only by your IP address.

This anonymity can be a resource, a refuge. The chat room can be its opposite, in a good way: a way of finding people like you, subcultures, when you can't find them geographically next door. But the internet has also intensified sex work backlash in the form of whore-shaming. It is as anonymous men at home on their computers, or anonymous men talking with other anonymous men in their Reddit forum, that many users flame and troll women in the public sphere, especially this Madonna/whore. The intense scrutiny of a woman's appearance, the intense dissection of her body, often accompanied by gruesome fantasies of literal dissection: it is this emerging digital public sphere that makes something like typewriter keys feel soothing, nostalgic for a previous time period when the press moved more slowly, a time period of the daily newspaper rather than the 24/7 Cable News Network and certainly not the updated-every-millisecond Twittersphere.

Whoredom has been at the vanguard of technology. So has slut-shaming. Madonna's ambivalent historical references, the desire of her sound effects for a more analog, more touch-focused past, capture this tension: the hardships of hustling, the work of staying sexy.

*   *   *

Twenty years after the release of *Erotica*, Madonna was on stage in Tel Aviv at the start of her MDNA world tour. MDNA was her twelfth studio album, but it was her first since the debut album of another singer with whom she had received many comparisons: Lady Gaga, whose *The Fame* had appeared just a couple of months after Madonna's *Hard Candy*. It was also just a year after Gaga's second album, *Born This Way*. In Tel Aviv on opening night of her new tour, Madonna transitioned from singing her own "Express Yourself" to covering the title track of Gaga's most recent album, before returning to some lyrics of her own: *She's not me, she's not me, she's not me.*

As the news and video clips spread across the internet, Madonna's fans were quick to decode the message. Gaga's "Born This Way" had been accused of plagiarizing "Express Yourself," in particular the chord progressions that accompany each song's chorus (ironically, Madonna had originally been accused of similarities between "Express Yourself" and the Staple Singers' "Respect Yourself"). Madonna seemed to be calling out the similarities while also suggesting that Gaga had tried, but would never be able, to become Madonna herself. At this early stage in her career, it seemed Gaga had been taking plays from Madonna's book, inviting religious scandal, investing in spectacle, desiring an acting career. The alleged rivalry between them, though, was cast as more Elektra complex than sibling rivalry, an intergenerational struggle for originality and relevance. Madonna had herself modeled, only to usurp, a previous generation, notably drawing freely, if contradictorily, from the self-fashionings of Marilyn Monroe and Marlene Dietrich. But to lift the sound from an iconic Madonna song was, fans contended, going further than homage, not least because this homage was unrecognized. This was not flattery but theft.

The terms in which the debate ensued were indicative of the extent to which Madonna had arrived as a businesswoman. What Gaga had stolen, if she had stolen something, was not just a style, not just an aesthetic that drag queens, too, had been invited to imitate, but rather Madonna's private property. Her songs were not just her art but her possessions. Complicating the matter was that both businesswomen were on the same record label (Madonna's Maverick label founded to boost *Erotica* was now defunct). When the debate between artists is cast as a struggle over intellectual ownership, we are often invited into intense scrutiny of the art itself. Especially in a period in which most computers come with some audio editing or analysis software, fans were quick to dissect chords, tempos, time stamps, melodies. What that kind of technical analysis misses about each song, however, is what comes before them, in particular the range of artists and cultural influences and music stylings and canonical leitmotifs that had already shaped a song like "Express Yourself." I am not just thinking about a team of producers and musicians that makes a song that nonetheless ends up being sold under the proper name of an individual: Madonna or Lady Gaga. I'm thinking, more importantly, about the musicians and stylings that were already appropriated or remixed or sampled or imitated in Madonna's tracks, as I've explored in this chapter and the previous one. Songs are the products not just of artists but of cultures.

What comparing a song like "Express Yourself" with a song like "Born This Way" helps do, then, is compare the different cultures from which they come: both a culture of US dance/pop but now separated by a generation. What seems most consistent across both productions is the more fundamental appropriation Madonna learned to entrench with *Erotica*, which is, as I argued in the previous chapter, pop's appropriation of politics itself. "Born This Way" carries forward the color-blind politics of Madonna's "Vogue": instead of it making *no difference if you're black or white, if you're a boy or a girl*, Gaga has *Whether you're broke or evergreen, you're Black, white, beige, chola descent, you're Lebanese, you're Orient*. This is, arguably, more offensive. But more than for her aspirational racial inclusion, Gaga had invited comparison with Madonna because of her clear desire to write a gay anthem. Now, the mood has shifted. Instead of mourning her friends like Madonna had done with "In This Life," Gaga was celebrating life, the myriad ways in which people had been *born this way*.

"Born this way" had become a rallying cry during the fight for same-sex marriage, because it invited civil rights comparisons to race and racism: if people couldn't help their sexual orientation any more than the color of the skin into which they were born, then the government had an obligation to let them be. The apparently progressive analogy had the unusual capacity, to me, to offend both opponents of racism and of homophobia, simultaneously underestimating how deeply racism structures US culture and pathologizing sexuality as something divorced from the liberation of choice and desire. It marked, to me, how limited the queer movement's mainstream goals had become. This was a politics of being left alone, because we couldn't help ourselves, a freedom *from*. But activists of a previous moment in the height of the AIDS epidemic were asking for freedoms *to*: freedom to queer public institutions, freedom to access health care, freedom to sex and community and space. Rather than gay marriage, a freedom to be left alone in your private home, this earlier politics was about a right to riot in the streets.

Over the course of the generational shift since Madonna's *Erotica*, there have been gay policy wins like the nationwide decriminalization of gay marriage in 2016, just as there has been an explosion of gay representation in a mainstream media landscape; now, there's more than just *Will & Grace* up for a GLAAD award. But these progressions in some areas have often required regressions in others. Legal gay marriage has sometimes made the traditional family form seem like the only way to make kinship, to make community, to organize subcultural space. And more mainstream television has sometimes required de-radicalizing or sanitizing queer life, leading to less complicated storylines in the name of token representation. Madonna remains worth visiting because, in contrast to progress narratives that "it gets better," what may seem "in the past" can sometimes be more radical than what is in the present. However sentimental *Erotica* is, as I explored in Chapter 1, and however complicated its relations to the subcultures it mines are, as I explored in Chapter 2, Madonna's indexing of an earlier moment in queer life and politics is worth revisiting today.

At the same time, as I've explored in this chapter, we should also be a little skeptical of when politics becomes appropriated for business, especially in *Erotica*, the album that launched her label. When politics looks like a form of personal expression, then it fits neatly into a pop song's lyrics about love, desire, and relationships. But when politics is about collective action, organizing in the streets, and dismantling social institutions, then something more is needed, something that moves beyond the brand name Madonna. As a whore, Madonna knows how to sell and resell sex, particularly by changing its erotic clothes while sticking to her core brand. A brand is good for business, but it can be a barrier to politics.

Also Available in this Series

ALSO AVAILABLE IN THIS SERIES